New

C000067232

Edited by **Gordon Giles** September–December 2024

Ministries

15 The Chambers, Vineyard,
Abingdon OX14 3FE
+44 (0)1865 319700 | brf.org.uk

Bible Reading Fellowship is a charity (233280) and company limited by guarantee (301324), registered in England and Wales

ISBN 978 1 80039 267 0

Cover image: pexels.com/@myfoodie
Editor and contributor photos used with kind permission

Distributed in Australia by:
MediaCom Education Inc, PO Box 610, Unley, SA 5061
Tel: 1 800 811 311 | admin@mediacom.org.au

Distributed in New Zealand by:
Scripture Union Wholesale, PO Box 760, Wellington 6140
Tel: 04 385 0421 | suwholesale@clear.net.nz

Acknowledgements
Scripture quotations marked with the following abbreviations are taken from the version shown. Where no abbreviation is given, the quotation is taken from the same version as the headline reference. **NIV**: The Holy Bible, New International Version, Anglicised edition, copyright © 1979, 1984, 2011 by Biblica. Used by permission of Hodder & Stoughton Publishers, an Hachette UK company. All rights reserved. 'NIV' is a registered trademark of Biblica. UK trademark number 1448790. **GNT**: the Good News Translation in Today's English Version – Second Edition Copyright © 1992 by American Bible Society. Used by Permission. **KJV**: The Authorised Version of the Bible (The King James Bible), the rights in which are vested in the Crown, are reproduced by permission of the Crown's Patentee, Cambridge University Press. **CEV**: the Contemporary English Version. New Testament © American Bible Society 1991, 1992, 1995. Old Testament © American Bible Society 1995. Anglicisations © British & Foreign Bible Society 1996. Used by permission. **NRSV**: the New Revised Standard Version Updated Edition. Copyright © 2021 National Council of Churches of Christ in the United States of America. Used by permission. All rights reserved worldwide.

A catalogue record for this book is available from the British Library

Printed and bound in the UK by Zenith Media NP4 0DQ

Suggestions for using *New Daylight*

Find a regular time and place, if possible, where you can read and pray undisturbed. Before you begin, take time to be still and perhaps use the prayer of BRF Ministries on page 6. Then read the Bible passage slowly (try reading it aloud if you find it over-familiar), followed by the comment. You can also use *New Daylight* for group study and discussion, if you prefer.

The prayer or point for reflection can be a starting point for your own meditation and prayer. Many people like to keep a journal to record their thoughts about a Bible passage and items for prayer. In *New Daylight* we also note the Sundays and some special festivals from the church calendar, to keep in step with the Christian year.

New Daylight and the Bible

New Daylight contributors use a range of Bible versions, and you will find a list of the versions used opposite. You are welcome to use your own preferred version alongside the passage printed in the notes. This can be particularly helpful if the Bible text has been abridged.

New Daylight affirms that the whole of the Bible is God's revelation to us, and we should read, reflect on and learn from every part of both Old and New Testaments. Usually the printed comment presents a straightforward 'thought for the day', but sometimes it may also raise questions rather than simply providing answers, as we wrestle with some of the more difficult passages of scripture.

New Daylight is also available in a deluxe edition (larger format). Visit your local Christian bookshop or BRF's online shop **brfonline.org.uk**. To obtain an audio version for the blind or partially sighted, contact Torch Trust for the Blind, Torch House, Torch Way, Northampton Road, Market Harborough LE16 9HL; +44 (0)1858 438260; **info@torchtrust.org**.

Comment on *New Daylight*

To send feedback, please email **enquiries@brf.org.uk**, phone **+44 (0)1865 319700** or write to the address shown opposite.

Writers in this issue

Steve Aisthorpe is the director of Kilmalieu, a place of prayer, hospitality and nature on the west coast of Scotland. He is the author of *The Invisible Church* and *Rewilding the Church*.

Amanda Bloor is archdeacon of Cleveland in the diocese of York, and has previously been a bishop's chaplain, a diocesan director of ordinands, an advisor in women's ministry and a parish priest.

Paul Gravelle (1931–2023) was an Anglican priest in Auckland, New Zealand, as well as a poet, writer and retreat leader. (*See the interview with Paul, and the editor's note, on page 147.*)

Margot Hodson is theology and education director for the John Ray Initiative. She is also a vicar in the Oxford diocese. **Martin Hodson** is a plant scientist and environmental biologist and teaches at both universities in Oxford. The Hodsons have published widely together on Christianity and the environment, including *A Christian Guide to Environmental Issues* (BRF, 2021).

Andy John was elected bishop of Bangor in 2008 and archbishop of Wales in 2021. His main interests include sports of most kinds and walking in the hills on North Wales, although has been known occasionally to indulge his terrible taste in music on a rickety old electric guitar.

Stephen Rand worked with Tearfund and Open Doors, travelling widely. He established advocacy and campaigning at both organisations. Now retired, he is part of the church leadership team of Orchard Baptist Church in Bicester, Oxfordshire.

Amy Scott Robinson is the author of several books, including *Image of the Invisible* and *Images of Grace*, a regular contributor to *Church Times*, and works as commissioning editor for children's and youth at Kevin Mayhew.

Margaret Silf is an ecumenical Christian committed to working across and beyond traditional divisions. She is the author of a number of books for 21st-century spiritual pilgrims and a retreat facilitator.

Veronica Zundel is an Oxford graduate, writer and columnist. She lives with her husband and son in North London. Her book *Everything I Know about God, I've Learned from Being a Parent* was published by BRF in 2013.

Gordon Giles writes...

Beethoven's Fifth Symphony begins with just four notes, which form the basis of the first movement of perhaps the most famous symphony there is. From that little phrase, which lasts about a second, comes seven-and-a-half minutes of music.

From a small start something big can burgeon. A symphony, a large painting, a great novel or indeed a human being: everything must start somewhere, somewhere small. From a single cell emerges so much – all life in fact.

Jesus described a mustard seed as the miniscule basis of something large. Similarly Peter's brief statement of faith, when he declared Jesus to be the Messiah, turned out to be huge. For the church started out small. Small is beautiful, and small is just the first stage of big. The Big Bang of creation was a very small thing that literally exploded into something massive which is still expanding, growing.

The earthly church, emergent from the singularity of Jesus himself, currently stands at 2,173,180,000 Christians, which is 31% of the world population. Half are Roman Catholic and 37% Protestant (including the Anglican Communion), 12% Orthodox and 1% other.

There are 1.5 billion Muslims and nearly 14 million Jews, 80% of whom live in Israel or the USA, while 1.2 billion people have no religious affiliation. Just over a billion are Hindus, 94% of which live in India. There are half a billion Buddhists, half of whom live in China. Christianity is not a minority nor is it in decline. According to recent surveys, by 2050 the number of Christians will reach 3 billion (which will be 31.4% of the world's population) and by 2060 Christians will still form the world's largest religion when the number will reach 3.05 billion (or 31.8%). Of course, this is not a numbers game, but the numbers do give us a sense of perspective, and crucially a sense of how much has expanded from what seems so little.

The journey of faith is one of growth. The story of Christianity is one of small beginnings and great growth, which in us and through us can be a burgeoning of faith, hope and love, for ourselves and others. A little trust in God, belief in Jesus, kindness to others and humility make up a small opening which can grow into a symphony of faith, hope and love.

GORDON GILES

The prayer of BRF Ministries

Faithful God,
thank you for growing BRF
from small beginnings
into the worldwide family of BRF Ministries.
We rejoice as young and old
discover you through your word
and grow daily in faith and love.
Keep us humble in your service,
ambitious for your glory
and open to new opportunities.
For your name's sake,
Amen.

'It is such a joy to be part of this amazing project'

As part of our Living Faith ministry, we're raising funds to give away copies of Bible reading notes and other resources to those who aren't able to access them any other way, working with food banks and chaplaincy services, in prisons, hospitals and care homes.

'This very generous gift will be hugely appreciated, and truly bless each recipient… Bless you for your kindness.'

'We would like to send our enormous thanks to all involved. Your generosity will have a significant impact and will help us to continue to provide support to local people in crisis, and for this we cannot thank you enough.'

If you've enjoyed and benefited from our resources, would you consider paying it forward to enable others to do so too?

Make a gift at **brf.org.uk/donate**

Harvest

 I grew up in Birmingham. I did not know anyone who ploughed the fields and scattered good seed on the land. As I got older I realised someone must be doing it on my behalf – in fact an enormous network of people across the world producing bananas from the Caribbean, coffee from Brazil, strawberries from Kent – and, of course, chocolate from Bournville, just down the road! All fed and watered by God's almighty hand.

Then I began work with Tearfund. Year after year I produced resources for harvest festivals. I discovered that most churches celebrated harvest on the last Sunday in September, earlier in Scotland because the harvest is earlier. I also discovered that fewer and fewer churches were holding harvest festivals.

And as I travelled to gather information for these harvest festival resources, I came face-to-face with people whose harvest had been destroyed by drought. I squatted in the dust beside a church elder as he gave thanks for a meal that consisted of leaves and berries gathered from the trees and boiled into an unappetising sticky black leafy dollop. Another visit, I woke one morning to hear the cries of wailing lament for those who had died of starvation in the night.

I wonder if you are among the dwindling number who still 'say grace' before a meal? I love the fact that it is called 'grace'. The prosaic reason is that it comes from the Latin word for giving thanks (in Italian, *grazie*). But it is also a reminder that our food – indeed all that we have, our life and breath – are a gift from God, one that we do not deserve. A short prayer before grasping the knife and fork can be a meaningless habit; it can also be the moment, daily, when we remember our interdependence as a human family and our dependence on a loving God who is worthy of our thanks.

A church harvest festival can perform the same function in the life of the Christian community. Together we celebrate all the resources that God gives us to sustain our life. And we give thanks.

'Give us today our daily bread' (Matthew 6:11, NIV). For the next two weeks celebrate a harvest festival with me, in small, hopefully meaningful, bite-sized pieces of daily bread.

STEPHEN RAND

The promise of harvest

The Lord smelled the pleasing aroma and said in his heart: 'Never again will I curse the ground because of humans, even though every inclination of the human heart is evil from childhood. And never again will I destroy all living creatures, as I have done. As long as the earth endures, seedtime and harvest, cold and heat, summer and winter, day and night will never cease.'

Noah's ark is a great story and a Sunday school staple. The problem is that you have to gloss over the almost total destruction of humankind. It is not easy for a five-year-old to grasp the concept of God's judgement and mercy; it is perhaps no easier for a 75-year-old.

But now there is the growing evidence of a new threat to the existence of humankind. Floods, heatwaves, droughts: extreme weather events that indicate the reality of global warming and climate change caused by human activity, the burning of fossil fuels. Politicians dither, on the one hand promoting policies in pursuit of net zero and then terrified that interfering with voters' driving habits will lose them support in the next election.

God's promise in Genesis is that he will never again destroy life: seedtime and harvest will never cease. Right now we face the challenge – do we trust God to keep his promise?

When the Israelites were freed from Egypt and travelling in the wilderness, God provided a daily harvest of manna. They were instructed to only take enough for each day. Those who did not trust God to provide the next day and took more than enough discovered that it went rotten: greed stinks.

In 2024 the earth still produces enough food to feed all its eight billion inhabitants: God is keeping his promise. But it is conditional: it is for 'as long as the earth endures'. God alone knows how long that will be. And the Bible is clear that he alone will decide when it is time for 'a new heaven and a new earth'. In the meantime, every Christian should be concerned to take care of the planet, of God's creation, for the sake of the one who made it and for the good of all who share it.

Almighty God, thank you for your promise of harvest;
help me to receive it carefully, wisely and generously. Amen.

STEPHEN RAND

Three harvest festivals

'Three times a year you are to celebrate a festival to me. Celebrate the Festival of Unleavened Bread; for seven days eat bread made without yeast, as I commanded you. Do this at the appointed time in the month of Aviv, for in that month you came out of Egypt. No one is to appear before me empty-handed. Celebrate the Festival of Harvest with the firstfruits of the crops you sow in your field. Celebrate the Festival of Ingathering at the end of the year, when you gather in your crops from the field.'

The Israelites entered the promised land with instructions to hold three harvest festivals – and two of them lasted for a week! That is certainly some celebrating.

Each time, the men were required to gather, which may explain why the festivals were held when the work of harvest was complete. And they were not only focused on harvest; they were to remember what God had done for them. The harvest offerings were a reminder of what God was *still* doing for them: he had acted in the past to set them free; he was acting in the present by sustaining their life through the harvest.

The Festival of Unleavened Bread began with the solemn celebration of Passover, the annual reminder of the exodus, the liberation of God's people. It came at the end of the barley harvest, and everyone was required to bring some barley with them.

The Festival of Harvest came 50 days later; this time it was the wheat harvest that was a key part of the celebration. Two loaves of leavened bread were waved by the priest before God and the people. We know this festival better as Pentecost. It commemorated the giving of the law at Mount Sinai, the day the fire of God came down and God spoke to all the people.

The Festival of Ingathering, the Feast of Shelters, or Tabernacles, came after the grape harvest. As they celebrated the fruits of their labour, the people were told to be joyous.

So the three great sacred festivals all had a harvest dimension. Then, as now, God provides, and is worthy of thanks.

Generous God, we rejoice in your provision:
for what we receive each day, we are truly thankful. Amen.

STEPHEN RAND

Firstfruits

The Lord said to Moses, 'Speak to the Israelites and say to them: "When you enter the land I am going to give you and you reap its harvest, bring to the priest a sheaf of the first grain you harvest. He is to wave the sheaf before the Lord so it will be accepted on your behalf; the priest is to wave it on the day after the Sabbath…. From the day after the Sabbath, the day you brought the sheaf of the wave offering, count off seven full weeks. Count off fifty days up to the day after the seventh Sabbath, and then present an offering of new grain to the Lord. From wherever you live, bring two loaves made of one fifth of an ephah of the finest flour, baked with yeast, as a wave offering of firstfruits to the Lord."'

It must have been quite a spectacle. Suddenly a sheaf of grain, or two large loaves of bread, would be lifted high in the air and then waved from side to side for all to see. It certainly would have been noticeable. I do not think anyone is sure of the significance of the waving, but here is my tentative suggestion: it was an offering, not a sacrifice, lifted up and presented to God because it was his; received back by the priest and used as food by him, recognising that God had provided for him.

Notice that in the Israelite harvest festivals, the offering to God came first – the firstfruits were his. There was no waiting to see if they had enough; no scraping up the leftovers.

I have a friend who was without work, down to his last few pence, when he went to church and heard the preacher challenge everyone to make sure that they honoured God and gave to him first, before anything was spent on themselves. He felt he had heard God speak. He emptied his pockets on to the plate, and he went home to bed literally penniless. The very next day he was offered a job, and he worked his way to the top, eventually taking over the company. That Sunday evening his life was turned around. He put God first.

All we have comes from God and belongs to God.

STEPHEN RAND

Caring for the land

The Lord said to Moses… 'When you enter the land I am going to give you, the land itself must observe a sabbath to the Lord. For six years sow your fields, and for six years prune your vineyards and gather their crops. But in the seventh year… Do not sow your fields or prune your vineyards. Do not reap what grows of itself or harvest the grapes of your untended vines. The land is to have a year of rest… Whatever the land produces may be eaten… Follow my decrees and be careful to obey my laws… Then the land will yield its fruit, and you will eat your fill… You may ask, "What will we eat in the seventh year if we do not plant or harvest our crops?" I will send you such a blessing in the sixth year that the land will yield enough for three years.'

I enjoy TV programmes that take you inside the factory, particularly those where food is produced. Perhaps it is the result of my first paid employment: a holiday job at Cadbury's. (I will not forget the joy of the broken conveyor belt creating a 15-foot mountain of chocolate buttons!) The sheer volume of ingredients and production is awe-inspiring – six million Jaffa cakes produced every day. Agriculture has become a massive business, as it must if eight billion people are to be fed.

When the Israelites reached their promised land, each family took responsibility for a plot. They were stewards, not owners – the land belonged to God (see Psalm 24:1) and they were to look after it, not exploit it. They were subsistence farmers, reliant on the land for their daily bread. It was their resource for sustaining life.

The promise was clear, however: do what you are asked, and all will be well.

Apparently modern experts indicate that giving the land a rest is good for its productivity. But then it is not surprising that the God who made the land knows how best to care for it. One of the underlying principles of Old Testament law is protection against over-exploitation – of land as well as of people.

Living in God's world God's way is not only right,
but good for all.

STEPHEN RAND

Sharing the harvest

When you are harvesting in your field and you overlook a sheaf, do not go back to get it. Leave it for the foreigner, the fatherless and the widow, so that the Lord your God may bless you in all the work of your hands. When you beat the olives from your trees, do not go over the branches a second time. Leave what remains for the foreigner, the fatherless and the widow. When you harvest the grapes in your vineyard, do not go over the vines again. Leave what remains for the foreigner, the fatherless and the widow. Remember that you were slaves in Egypt. That is why I command you to do this.

These subsistence farmers had to take care not only of the land, but also of other people, those outside their own family. Throughout the books of the law there are regular mentions of the foreigner, the fatherless and the widow. What links these three very different groups of people? They were those without access to land on which they could grow their own food – they depended on others for their sustenance.

So God insists that the whole agricultural system has to work to include the outsiders and to ensure that no one becomes hungry or destitute. This is a thread woven into the whole fabric of Old Testament law. The specific instruction given in Leviticus 23:22 – 'When you reap the harvest of your land, do not reap to the very edges of your field or gather the gleanings of your harvest. Leave them for the poor and for the foreigner residing among you' – is the basis of the story of Ruth, which reveals the generosity and thoughtfulness with which these laws could shape relationships and community.

Some view it as hopelessly romantic and inefficient. Some argue that it was never really worked out in practice. But the basic concern enshrined in God's instructions still informs Christian action on behalf of the vulnerable. There should be no need for food banks in 2024, but it is no accident that churches are at the heart of this network of care for the needy.

Harvests come as a blessing from God, and blessings are given to be shared.

God, let me be open-handed, not tight-fisted. Amen.

STEPHEN RAND

Sow generously, reap thanksgiving

Remember this: whoever sows sparingly will also reap sparingly, and whoever sows generously will also reap generously. Each of you should give what you have decided in your heart to give, not reluctantly or under compulsion, for God loves a cheerful giver. And God is able to bless you abundantly, so that in all things at all times, having all that you need, you will abound in every good work… Now he who supplies seed to the sower and bread for food will also supply and increase your store of seed and will enlarge the harvest of your righteousness. You will be enriched in every way so that you can be generous on every occasion, and through us your generosity will result in thanksgiving to God.

Paul was steeped in the law of Moses. As he shaped the life and practice of the first Christian communities, he insisted that they were 'not under law, but under grace' (Romans 6:14) on the understanding that the behaviour the law had demanded would now be a harvest of the fruit of the Spirit.

So when famine struck one of the new Christian communities, Paul set up an emergency relief fund and wrote appeal letters to the others to encourage generous giving. Today's reading is part of the one sent to the church in Corinth. Paul's focus is on what will be achieved by their giving: it will be good for those in need, and it will be good for them. They will be blessed, he says, so that they can be generous. The more generous they are, the more they will be blessed. The more they give, the more they will have to give. It is not a guide to how to become wealthy, but how to stay generous.

I met Tiekle in Ethiopia at the height of the famine there in 1984. She was 20-years-old, and had carried her baby 250 miles in search of food. She did not know if she would ever see her husband again. With eyes full of tears, she said, 'We thank God for the help you have brought.' Generosity had resulted in thanksgiving to God.

How cheerful is your giving?
Do you focus on its cost to you or the benefits it will bring to others?

STEPHEN RAND

A harvest for the family

Do not deceive yourselves; no one makes a fool of God. You will reap exactly what you plant. If you plant in the field of your natural desires, from it you will gather the harvest of death; if you plant in the field of the Spirit, from the Spirit you will gather the harvest of eternal life. So let us not become tired of doing good; for if we do not give up, the time will come when we will reap the harvest. So then, as often as we have the chance, we should do good to everyone, and especially to those who belong to our family in the faith.

Paul loved using agricultural analogies! Here is another example of his use of the imagery of sowing and reaping as a picture of life and spiritual reality. Just as you cannot grow apples from orange pips, so you cannot expect to live life with God if your focus is on living for yourself.

Many people try to have it both ways: they hope that if they squeeze God and his way of living into a corner of their weekly routine, he will be kind enough to overlook being marginalised most of the time. But no one can fool God; as the King James Version puts it, 'God is not mocked' (v. 7).

These verses are written in the context of Paul describing how members of the Christian community should behave towards one another. 'Carry one another's burdens', says verse 2. I am sure Paul knew just how demanding and/or difficult fellow Christians could be, yet he encourages us to not become 'tired of doing good' (v. 9).

Paul is clear that we should care not just for our fellow Christians; our love and kindness should extend to all. But he describes the Christian community as a family, those with whom we have a special relationship.

My experience with the work of Open Doors revealed to me that one of the forms of persecution faced by Christians in many countries was discrimination, including being overlooked in the distribution of emergency relief supplies. It was an opportunity to do good to those who are part of our family of faith.

---

*Lord Jesus, when I'm tired out by caring for others, grant me
renewed energy and deeper reserves of loving kindness. Amen.*

STEPHEN RAND

The cries of the harvesters

Now listen, you rich people, weep and wail because of the misery that is coming on you… Look! The wages you failed to pay the workers who mowed your fields are crying out against you. The cries of the harvesters have reached the ears of the Lord Almighty. You have lived on earth in luxury and self-indulgence. You have fattened yourselves in the day of slaughter.

It is almost impossible to believe that these angry words are part of the New Testament. It is as if an Old Testament prophet has become a left-wing agitator. I suspect if I shouted these words in a street in the City of London it might not be long before the police arrived.

But as those who have largely benefited from capitalism, it is easy to forget that the Bible consistently reminds us that God is deeply concerned about how wealth is gained and how it is used. And it is easy to forget that poverty itself is the result of the failure to live up to God's standards: 'There need be no poor people among you… if only you fully obey the Lord your God and are careful to follow all these commands I am giving you today' (Deuteronomy 15:4–5).

I once visited an area in Bangladesh that included a British-owned tea estate. Its workers were foreigners who had been moved there under the Raj and now in effect imprisoned on the estate. They were significantly poorer than the local Bengalis; there was a high incidence of leprosy, a significant sign of poverty. The management of the estate said they could not afford to pay the staff more, as the tea would become too expensive. But I noted that the shareholders were still receiving their annual dividend.

That experience has helped me remain committed to the Fairtrade movement over most of my adult life, campaigning for our church(es) and town to share in that commitment and ensure that the people who grow our food are properly rewarded. And last year the signs went up on all the roads into Bicester, proclaiming it to be a Fairtrade town. We *can* hear the cries of those who gather in our crops – and do something about it.

Father, keep me mindful of all those
who labour so that I can eat. Amen.

STEPHEN RAND

An inspiring vision

'See, I will create new heavens and a new earth… Be glad and rejoice forever in what I will create, for I will create Jerusalem to be a delight and its people a joy… They will build houses and dwell in them… plant vineyards and eat their fruit. No longer will they build houses and others live in them, or plant and others eat. For as the days of a tree, so will be the days of my people; my chosen ones will long enjoy the work of their hands. They will not labour in vain, nor bear children doomed to misfortune; for they will be a people blessed by the Lord.'

Isaiah paints this powerful and inspiring picture of how God intends the world to be. It is infused with words of uplift and beauty: delight, joy, blessed. Yet it is rooted in the experience of poverty shared by millions across the world. Years ago I saw the appalling living conditions of the families of the men building a luxury hotel. Millions grow food for others to eat and scarcely have enough themselves.

Isaiah's vision is not of Shangri-la (earthly paradise) – idleness and pleasure. Rather, it speaks of purpose, fulfilment and satisfaction. You will have had a glimpse of this when you have cooked a lovely meal, knitted a beautiful pullover, grown your own tomatoes, decorated a room or written a poem. I am so grateful to God that when I held my daughters as newborn babies, I knew they were not 'doomed to misfortune' (v. 23).

'Count your blessings', wrote Johnson Oatman in his 1897 hymn. It should have a sequel: 'Share your blessings.' Then there will be a 'harvest of righteousness'. This vision was not given so that we could sit back, relax and wait for God to deliver on his promise. It is like the picture on the jigsaw puzzle box – a guide to how things will look if all the pieces are set in their rightful place. If I can live in such a way that I put just one piece in the right place in God's picture of joy and perfection – what a privilege, what an opportunity!

Lord, keep inspiring me with your vision
of how the world should be. Amen.

STEPHEN RAND

Sow in peace

Who is wise and understanding among you? Let them show it by their good life, by deeds done in the humility that comes from wisdom. But if you harbour bitter envy and selfish ambition in your hearts, do not boast about it or deny the truth. Such 'wisdom' does not come down from heaven but is earthly, unspiritual, demonic. For where you have envy and selfish ambition, there you find disorder and every evil practice. But the wisdom that comes from heaven is first of all pure; then peace-loving, considerate, submissive, full of mercy and good fruit, impartial and sincere. Peacemakers who sow in peace reap a harvest of righteousness.

Today, it is James who is contrasting good and bad behaviour – and he is also drawn to the parallel of the harvest, even reaching the conclusion with the same phrase: 'a harvest of righteousness' (v. 18).

James was a key leader in the church in Jerusalem. Much of his letter is focused on how Christians should relate to one another. He was no stranger to this challenge. In Acts 15 and 21 he is centrally involved in resolving the issue that threatened to tear the church apart in its earliest years: to what extent should non-Jews who become Christian adopt Jewish practices? The leadership he shows demonstrates the very qualities he is writing about here: it is full of wisdom, considerate and sincere, and above all peace-loving.

What is more, the results illustrate the truth of the proverb. The decision of the Council of Jerusalem, following James' leadership, is wonderfully fruitful as the church grows rapidly among non-Jews while holding on to its unity (see Acts 15).

There are issues threatening to tear churches apart today. At a national and local level James' wisdom of leadership is needed more than ever. Sadly, debates are not always peace-loving; the loudest voices are sometimes divisive and angry rather than submissive and full of mercy. This may bear fruit, but not a harvest of righteousness: people turn away from the church, and a whole generation may miss the opportunity of finding a relationship with Jesus in the fellowship of his people.

Sowing is a positive action of hope. Where, right now,
can you sow in peace? Jesus said, 'Blessed are the peacemakers.'

STEPHEN RAND

The parable of the sower

'This is the meaning of the parable: the seed is the word of God. Those along the path are the ones who hear, and then the devil comes and takes away the word from their hearts, so that they may not believe and be saved. Those on the rocky ground are the ones who receive the word with joy when they hear it, but they have no root. They believe for a while, but in the time of testing they fall away. The seed that fell among thorns stands for those who hear, but as they go on their way they are choked by life's worries, riches and pleasures, and they do not mature. But the seed on good soil stands for those with a noble and good heart, who hear the word, retain it, and by persevering produce a crop.'

I grew up in a church where preachers in the evening 'gospel service' often chose the parable of the sower as their topic. The assumption was there would be people present who had not heard the good news of Jesus, or who had not yet responded to it. So the preacher would encourage the listener to consider what kind of soil they were. Were they ready and willing to hear the word, retain it and persevere?

Those preachers of my youth quoted Matthew 13:23 – 'This is the one who produces a crop, yielding a hundred, sixty or thirty times what was sown' – and assumed it meant that once someone became a Christian, they would encourage others to do the same. That understanding must have greatly encouraged those first disciples! They were a tiny persecuted minority; I doubt they imagined that one day a third of the world would be followers of Jesus.

There is another interpretation. When someone truly receives the word of God in their life, the result is the harvest fruit of the Spirit. As James 2:14 puts it: 'What good is it for one of you to say that you have faith if your actions do not prove it?' (GNT). Of course, the two interpretations merge: if my life displays the fruit of the Spirit, others will want to know more about the good news of Jesus.

Lord, help me by your Spirit to produce a good crop. Amen.

STEPHEN RAND

Workers in the harvest field

After this the Lord appointed seventy-two others and sent them two by two ahead of him to every town and place where he was about to go. He told them, 'The harvest is plentiful, but the workers are few. Ask the Lord of the harvest, therefore, to send out workers into his harvest field. Go! I am sending you out like lambs among wolves. Do not take a purse or bag or sandals; and do not greet anyone on the road. When you enter a house, first say, "Peace to this house."'

There is a job to be done! Jesus is clear that it will not be easy to work in the harvest field of the mission of the church. There can be no distractions or encumbrances, but the goal is to bring God's peace. What an incentive, and what a privilege!

Matthew's gospel sets this request for labourers in the context of a summary of the ministry of Jesus, a sort of blueprint (see Matthew 9:35–38). Nowhere and no one was excluded. It was holistic: teaching, to involve the mind and encourage understanding; preaching, to engage the spirit and provoke a response; healing, restoring the body and establishing well-being. It was rooted in compassion, love for those made in the image of God but who were lost and broken.

Today, as then, the harvest is plentiful. There is no shortage of opportunity to share the love of God in word and deed, but the workers are still few. These verses can encourage people to become overseas missionaries. But every Christian is called to be a worker, every church is an outreach outpost in the harvest field.

I once met a woman who could not bear to watch the news. So much suffering; she felt helpless, she could do nothing to make a difference. Then she heard there were Christians working to feed the hungry, to stand with the vulnerable, to show love to the marginalised and oppressed. So she started watching the news. Then she would switch it off and pray for the Christians making a difference in the places and situations that had been highlighted. She had become a worker in God's harvest field.

Father, give me the resources of courage, time, wisdom and, above all, love, so that I can be an effective worker in the harvest field. Amen.

STEPHEN RAND

Seize the time

Sow righteousness for yourselves, reap the fruit of unfailing love, and break up your unploughed ground; for it is time to seek the Lord, until he comes and showers his righteousness on you. But you have planted wickedness, you have reaped evil, you have eaten the fruit of deception. Because you have depended on your own strength and on your many warriors, the roar of battle will rise against your people.

What a beautiful exhortation from the prophet! In recent days we have reminded ourselves that it is God who provides the harvest and he wants us to share it. And when we share it, we are demonstrating the harvest, the fruit, that comes from the presence of God in our lives. Planting spiritual seed produces a harvest of love expressed in action as we become workers in God's harvest field, each with our own unique role to play.

Today's verses come like the closing passage of a sermon, a call for a response. God's word is there to be understood; it is there to be acted upon. It is time to seek the Lord! What does he want me to do? What does he want me to do less of, or more of? Or is there unploughed ground, somewhere new I should go, something new I should take on?

It is time to seek the Lord, because I cannot act in my own strength. That leads to strife, exhaustion and unproductiveness. I am aware of my age. The energy levels are not what they were! I look back over the years and thank God that though I have sometimes seen Christians at their worst, I have also met faithful followers of Jesus, unsung heroes, who have been empowered by God's Spirit to keep loving, to persevere, to make a difference.

I have been an activist, instinctively suspicious of those who seem to enjoy worship and contemplation but shun service. But I have learned that the mission of the church needs activists and it needs pray-ers; it needs people to work together, honouring and respecting what each person brings to the task. And activists need to seek the Lord; those who seek the Lord need to act on what he says!

'Plow your fields, scatter seeds of justice,
and harvest faithfulness' (Hosea 10:12, CEV).

STEPHEN RAND

A prayer for blessing

May God be gracious to us and bless us and make his face shine on us – so that your ways may be known on earth, your salvation among all nations. May the peoples praise you, God; may all the peoples praise you. May the nations be glad and sing for joy, for you rule the peoples with equity and guide the nations of the earth. May the peoples praise you, God; may all the peoples praise you. The land yields its harvest; God, our God, blesses us. May God bless us still, so that all the ends of the earth will fear him.

So we come full circle. We began with God's promise that seedtime and harvest would not cease. We finish with a hymn of prayer to God rooted in the fact of that promise being kept. Please bless us. We *are* blessed. Please keep blessing us.

This psalm is rooted in the reality consistently expressed in the Old Testament: God's people were a chosen people not only for their own blessing, but so that blessing could and would be seen and shared. Bless us, says the psalmist, 'so that your ways may be known on earth… May all the peoples praise you' (vv. 2–3). Being chosen by God was not his goal; it was his method to bless others.

For God's people today the message has not changed. We are blessed by God so that we can bless others. As we worship God, we long for others to join us. Christians have sought out the ends of the earth to share God's blessings.

Nearly 2,000 years ago, those who lived in the wealth and comfort of the heart of the known world set out to the heathen barbarians living in the cold and damp of the northern edge of civilisation and brought the good news of Jesus to Britannia. Britons still live in the benefit of that ancient act of obedience.

It has been a privilege to offer my thoughts to you through these daily readings. I hope and trust that what I have sown in writing will reap a harvest in your reading. Let me finish with my prayer for you today.

May God be gracious to you and bless you
and make his face shine on you. Amen.

STEPHEN RAND

John 8—10

Some years ago, my son undertook research to investigate 'design fixation'. This is the notion that, when people have pre-existing ideas in their mind, their ability to imagine new things is limited.

Let me explain. He gathered a group of people and asked them to create as many designs as possible for a non-spill coffee cup. Everyone received the same instructions except for one detail: the directions given to half the people included a picture of an existing design. The outcome was that those who saw that picture came up with significantly fewer new designs than the others. Their minds seemed to be impeded by that image in the instructions. The fact is that we easily get into ruts, which constrain our thinking and inhibit our ability to embrace change.

The central section of John's gospel includes a protracted series of arguments between Jesus and the religious leaders. It appears that they were shackled to well-established ways of thinking. They struggled to reconcile the claims and actions of Jesus with the narrative and understanding that already occupied their minds. Two millennia later, it is easy to judge the scribes and Pharisees as blinkered and dogmatic, but we should remember that we all struggle to adopt new ideas, especially when they relate to what is most precious to us. It is human nature.

We tend to think of the gospels as being packed with transformative encounters between Jesus and people he met, miracles and parables. These three chapters, close to the centre of John's account, are different. There is a miracle: a man born blind receives his sight. And, while there are no parables, Jesus does draw on some of the same imagery, especially sheep and shepherds. However, the constant backdrop is the heated debate over the assertions and activity of Jesus and repeated attempts to entrap him.

Those who listen to Jesus are often divided in their response. Some want to kill him. Others prostrate themselves in worship. We are told that many 'believed in him' and yet those people too appear to be unable to let go of established interpretations and embrace new perspectives. As we explore these chapters, let us pray for humility, approach with open minds and hearts, and allow the words and actions of Jesus to challenge and reshape us.

STEVE AISTHORPE

The scribes set a snare

The scribes and the Pharisees brought a woman who had been caught in adultery, and, making her stand before all of them, they said to him, 'Teacher, this woman was caught in the very act of committing adultery. Now in the law Moses commanded us to stone such women. Now what do you say?' They said this to test him… When they kept on questioning him, he straightened up and said to them, 'Let anyone among you who is without sin be the first to throw a stone at her.'

In chess it is known as a fork: one player moves a piece that threatens their opponent in multiple ways simultaneously. In today's passage, we sense the smugness and malice as the scribes and Pharisees spring a multifaceted trap to reveal this renegade rabbi as a heretic. It seems that the law is clear (Deuteronomy 22:22) and the evidence is conclusive. If Jesus condemns her, his growing reputation for compassion and being 'a friend of sinners' will be destroyed. If he does not, their suspicions that he is 'soft on crime' will be confirmed and everyone will see he treats the law with disdain. Surely, he is caught in an irreconcilable quandary.

Jesus responds: no words, no clever arguments and no dramatic action. Rather, mysteriously and to the exasperation of his antagonists, he stoops down and writes on the ground. Perhaps he is moved, distressed. To those who dragged her into the temple courts, the woman is 'an adultery case', but to Jesus she is a precious child of God. Broken, yes; guilty, probably; but also dearly loved and in need of a fresh start. Where is the love in this inhumane parading of the accused woman, and where is the man?

Then, straightening up, looking into the eyes of those who would accuse both the woman and him, Jesus delivers that single, chilling, disarming sentence: 'Let anyone among you who is without sin be the first to throw a stone at her' (v. 7). All are called to examine their own hearts and only then presume to engage in judging another. One moment bloodshed seems inevitable; in the next the older members of the crowd drift away, chastened, gradually followed by the rest.

Imagine yourself in the loving gaze of Jesus.
What does he say to you today?

STEVE AISTHORPE

Who do you think you are?

Again Jesus spoke to them, saying, 'I am the light of the world. Whoever follows me will never walk in darkness but will have the light of life.' Then the Pharisees said to him, 'You are testifying on your own behalf; your testimony is not valid.' Jesus answered, 'Even if I testify on my own behalf, my testimony is valid because I know where I have come from and where I am going'… He spoke these words while he was teaching in the treasury of the temple, but no one arrested him, because his hour had not yet come.

In these verses several themes that recur throughout John's gospel collide. First, we encounter one of Jesus' 'I am' statements. For people steeped in the Hebrew scriptures, that tiny phrase, 'I am', echoed God's revelation to Moses, 'I am who I am' (Exodus 3:14). Jesus' outrageous claim to be 'the light of the world' was intensified by the timing and venue. It was the Feast of Tabernacles, in the part of the temple that was illuminated dramatically during the celebrations. Who does this man think he is?

A second regular refrain in this gospel is the Pharisees' challenge to Jesus' legitimacy. Jesus was consistent and unwavering. His authority was from God and here he expresses that in terms of knowing both his origin and his destiny. He had come from the Father and would return to his side.

We encounter an example of a third theme in this gospel as we read that no one arrested him, 'because his hour had not yet come' (v. 20). Phrases like this punctuate John's gospel, creating the sense of a countdown towards a long-anticipated climax. An eternal plan is unfolding. At the wedding in Cana Jesus said, 'My hour has not yet come' (2:4). Seven times we are told, 'The hour is coming' (4:21, 23; 5:25, 28; 16:2, 25, 32). Then, as his death approached, Jesus prayed, 'Father, the hour has come' (17:1). Several times we hear conversations about his need to 'finish' the task his Father has given him to complete. Finally, from the cross, we hear, 'It is finished' (19:30).

Lord, I say 'yes' to your summons to follow.
When I think to myself 'Who do you think you are?',
remind me that I am loved by you and walk in your light. Amen.

STEVE AISTHORPE

The authorities are met with authority

They did not understand that he was speaking to them about the Father. So Jesus said, 'When you have lifted up the Son of Man, then you will realise that I am he and that I do nothing on my own, but I speak these things as the Father instructed me. And the one who sent me is with me; he has not left me alone, for I always do what is pleasing to him.' As he was saying these things, many believed in him.

The religious 'authorities' wrangle and wrestle with the one who speaks and acts with 'authority'. The Pharisees try to trap or trick. Jesus attempts to explain and enlighten. These few verses provide a microcosm of the response to Jesus both then and now: some 'do not understand' (v. 27) and others 'believe in him' (v. 31).

For the third time in this gospel, we hear Jesus talk of being 'lifted up'. There is a deliberate mixed meaning: he will be lifted up to die on a cross but also exalted and set in clear view. These are all interrelated aspects of God's plan for humankind and all creation. It will be as Jesus is physically lifted up, to suffer a prolonged and agonising death by crucifixion, that some will recognise who he is. There will be many who realise, like the Roman centurion on seeing Jesus 'lifted up', that 'truly this man was God's Son!' (Mark 15:39).

What a paradox! By means of an awful, tortuous execution, he will be exalted. By his submission, victory will come. Apparent weakness will be the means of God's ultimate demonstration of power and glory. Through the demise of God's Son, death will 'lose its sting' (1 Corinthians 15:55–57). All this will be possible because Jesus, and only Jesus, can claim 'I always do what is pleasing to him' (v. 29). His is a life of obedience and holiness. Throughout his disputing with the scribes and Pharisees, Jesus explains that he follows the Father's lead and is in perfect harmony with God.

We too are summoned to holiness. Through his example we are inspired. By his Spirit we are enabled.

Because he was 'lifted up' we can rejoice in the truth that
'there is now no condemnation for those who are in Christ Jesus'
(Romans 8:1).

STEVE AISTHORPE

Enduring faith or passing fad?

Then Jesus said to the Jews who had believed in him, 'If you continue in my word, you are truly my disciples, and you will know the truth, and the truth will make you free.' They answered him, 'We are descendants of Abraham and have never been slaves to anyone. What do you mean by saying, "You will be made free"?' Jesus answered them, 'Very truly, I tell you, everyone who commits sin is a slave to sin.'

After having been a follower of Jesus for only a few weeks, I went to a Bible study group, where I met a wonderful elderly man. Chatting afterwards, I explained how I seemed to be learning so much every day. He nodded sagely and responded, 'Me too!' I laughed. And then realised that he was serious, as he insisted that, after decades of discipleship, he continued to be encountering new truths, being challenged afresh and growing in faith and understanding. Now, some decades later, I know he was speaking the truth.

Among the crowds in the temple, some were convinced of their own truth and came to expose Jesus as a fraud. However, others 'believed in him', and it is to these people Jesus now turns. Like the seed that fell on rocky ground in the parable of the sower (Matthew 13:5), those who 'believed in him' made a promising start. Like all of us, they had questions. Questions and doubts are an integral part of the journey of faith and taking these to the Lord is a vital first step. Finding opportunities to discuss and explore them with others is also important.

In his gospel and letters, John reminds us regularly of the importance of 'continuing in the word', 'walking in the truth' and 'remaining' in Christ. Sadly, as Jesus' interactions with these people continues, we realise that humility and openness were lacking. Like that seed on stony ground, their commitment was fleeting and their potential for fruitfulness unfulfilled. Perhaps they were willing to accept Jesus as a teacher, but not as Lord. Maybe they liked what they heard but accepted it only as an addition to their existing beliefs.

We cannot follow Jesus on our own terms.
Cultivating an attitude that is teachable is vital.
Are you ready to embrace challenge and change?

STEVE AISTHORPE

The battle for our allegiance

They said to him, 'We are not illegitimate children; we have one Father, God himself.' Jesus said to them, 'If God were your Father, you would love me, for I came from God, and now I am here. I did not come on my own, but he sent me. Why do you not understand what I say? It is because you cannot accept my word. You are from your father the devil, and you choose to do your father's desires. He was a murderer from the beginning and does not stand in the truth because there is no truth in him.'

The debating and disputing continue. The people quarrelling with Jesus are religious people. They have come to the temple to celebrate the festival. They appear to be from the 'Jews who had believed in him' (8:31) and people who identify God as their Father. At a previous festival, we also read of people who believed in Jesus and yet he would not entrust himself to them because he 'knew what was in their hearts' (John 2:25, GNT). Jesus looks beyond affiliations, labels and identities to the heart. His offer of 'freedom' (8:32) remains, but it is not based on religious piety. Nor is it inherited because of ethnicity or ancestry. It is a gift, freely available, always received by empty hands, and by those who recognise their absolute inability to earn God's grace.

This feels like a harsh passage. Calling people 'children of the devil' may seem incompatible with what we know of Jesus, but he is explaining the incongruity of declaring devotion to God and lacking love for himself. Different 'fathers' vie for our devotion. The attributes of one are embodied perfectly in Jesus, from whom love and truth shine; the other is characterised by murder and lies.

Jesus peals back the pious camouflage and exposes the source of their thoughts, words and deeds. If what is revealed includes lies and conspiracy to murder, then any claims to be rooted in God are at best a wishful fiction. As we progress through this gospel, we learn that people's response to Jesus is a touchstone, a reflection of their standing with God.

'Create in me a clean heart, O God,
and put a new and right spirit within me' (Psalm 51:10). Amen.

STEVE AISTHORPE

Whose fault is this?

As he walked along, he saw a man blind from birth. His disciples asked him, 'Rabbi, who sinned, this man or his parents, that he was born blind?' Jesus answered, 'Neither this man nor his parents sinned; he was born blind so that God's works might be revealed in him. We must work the works of him who sent me while it is day; night is coming, when no one can work. As long as I am in the world, I am the light of the world.'

The first half of John's gospel has been called the Book of Signs. After turning water into wine, we are told, 'Jesus did this, the first of his signs… and revealed his glory' (John 2:11). Six other 'signs' follow, including this healing of the blind man. The verses that follow tell us that Jesus 'made mud with the saliva' and spread it on the man's eyes and, after washing in the pool of Siloam, the man returned 'able to see'.

These signs reveal who Jesus is. Later, John is unapologetic and explicit about why, out of the masses of Jesus' miracles and teaching, he selected what he did for inclusion in this gospel: 'These are written so that you may continue to believe that Jesus is the Messiah, the Son of God, and that through believing you may have life in his name' (20:31).

The disciples used the opportunity of meeting the blind man to ask a variant of the perennial question, 'Why suffering?' Their question revealed an underlying assumption, the idea that an individual's suffering could be attributed to some specific sin. Jesus was unequivocal in stating that this was neither a general principle nor an explanation for this man's blindness. He refused to attribute blame.

The scriptures remind us that the world was not always home to suffering. In the beginning, 'God saw everything that he had made, and indeed, it was very good' (Genesis 1:31). We can also be confident that suffering is temporary. A day is coming when 'mourning and crying and pain will be no more' (Revelation 21:4). However, we live in the in-between time.

The mystery and misery of suffering is a harsh reality,
but the compassion and power of Jesus brings forgiveness,
healing and 'signs' of the new era to come.

STEVE AISTHORPE

Jesus' actions bring division

They brought to the Pharisees the man who had formerly been blind. Now it was a Sabbath day when Jesus made the mud and opened his eyes. Then the Pharisees also began to ask him how he had received his sight. He said to them, 'He put mud on my eyes. Then I washed, and now I see.' Some of the Pharisees said, 'This man is not from God, for he does not observe the Sabbath.' Others said, 'How can a man who is a sinner perform such signs?' And they were divided.

'Word spread like wildfire' is a phrase that existed long before mobile phones and social media. News of the astounding transformation of a well-known local character was on everyone's lips within minutes. However, instead of prompting rejoicing, his healing provoked consternation and debate, as people wondered how this was possible and what it could mean. In such a deeply devout society, it was natural to look to the Pharisees for a judgement.

To understand the significance of the restoration of the man's sight taking place on the sabbath, we need to look back to chapter 5. Jesus had already incurred the wrath of religious leaders by healing a man who had been crippled for nearly 40 years, even claiming to be 'lord of the Sabbath' (Matthew 12:8). Their anger was exacerbated when, in justifying his actions, Jesus claimed he was following the Father's lead, acting in the authority given to him by God: 'My Father is still working, and I also am working' (John 5:17), even on the sabbath.

This time the Pharisees began their investigation by interrogating the previously blind man. It is striking how his simple, unembellished account cuts through the theological wrangling. However, those who heard it and witnessed the reality of his restored vision were divided. To people zealous for the law, the evidence seemed to conflict. The miracle itself was staggering. The only time anyone had heard of such a thing was in the writings of the prophets. Was it not a sign of the long-awaited Messiah that 'the eyes of the blind shall be opened' (Isaiah 35:5)? And yet, how could a man who treated their sabbath regulations with indifference be from God?

Lord, please help me to share my own faith story
with uncomplicated candour. Amen.

STEVE AISTHORPE

Suffering for doing right

The Jews did not believe that he had been blind and had received his sight until they called the parents of the man... His parents answered, 'We know that this is our son and that he was born blind, but we do not know how it is that now he sees, nor do we know who opened his eyes. Ask him; he is of age. He will speak for himself.' His parents said this because they were afraid of the Jews, for the Jews had already agreed that anyone who confessed Jesus to be the Messiah would be put out of the synagogue.

Having grilled the previously sightless man, the Pharisees turned their attention to his parents. Would they dare to corroborate his story? It appears that the parents' fear prompted an evasive response to the religious authorities.

In tightly knit, primarily agricultural societies, interdependence is crucial, and in first-century Palestine, affiliation with the local synagogue really mattered. The threat of expulsion that was hanging over anyone who expressed support for Jesus would be taken extremely seriously.

We are reminded here that suffering can sometimes result from doing the right thing, a fact that Jesus was clear about when he sent out the apostles. The parents thought they had sidestepped the ire of their inquisitors, but in fact it would be redirected on their son, who was then driven out.

To be called to follow Jesus is the ultimate privilege, but it also comes with a health warning. We are called to walk in the footsteps of the one the prophets depicted as a 'suffering servant'. In being entirely faithful to his Father, the Messiah would be 'a man of suffering, and familiar with pain' (Isaiah 53:3, NIV). Jesus likened his own mission and destiny to a grain of wheat falling to the ground and dying to make possible a bumper harvest. He was explicit in warning his followers that they were being sent out 'like sheep among wolves' and would be handed over to various authorities and suffer greatly (Matthew 10).

Lord, today we remember the estimated 360 million Christians around the world facing persecution. Support and strengthen them, please, and help me also to see where I am called to do the right thing regardless of repercussions. Amen.

STEVE AISTHORPE

The truth dawns, gradually

Jesus heard that they had driven him out, and when he found him he said, 'Do you believe in the Son of Man?' He answered, 'And who is he, sir? Tell me, so that I may believe in him.' Jesus said to him, 'You have seen him, and the one speaking with you is he.' He said, 'Lord, I believe.' And he worshipped him. Jesus said, 'I came into this world for judgement so that those who do not see may see and those who do see may become blind.'

'The Hound of Heaven', a poem by Francis Thompson (1859–1907), imagines the love of God pursuing the author's fleeing soul. The tenacious pursuit of a hound after a hare, the 'unhurrying chase and unperturbed pace', is a metaphor for God's persistent search for each of us, his longing to extend his grace to us, eager for restored relationship. This imagery may sound menacing, but it expresses the same yearning for reconciliation as the conscientious care of the shepherd who will 'leave the ninety-nine on the mountains and go in search of the one that went astray' (Matthew 18:12).

It is unusual in the gospels for Jesus to deliberately seek someone out. However, having heard that the man he had healed was now ostracised and expelled from the synagogue, Jesus tracked him down. His heart of compassion would not rest until they really saw one another for the first time.

If we look at the whole account of this healing and the ensuing investigations, we see how the man's understanding progresses gradually. First, he refers to his healer as 'the man called Jesus' (John 9:11). During his first interrogation, he identifies Jesus as 'a prophet' (v. 17). During his second grilling by the authorities, he recognises that Jesus is 'from God' (v. 33). Finally, beholding Jesus with his recently functioning eyes, he sees that Jesus is who he claims to be. The 'Son of Man' (v. 35) is a term in the Hebrew scriptures for the Messiah figure, the one invested with divine authority and glory (Daniel 7). Confronted by such a realisation, worship is the only appropriate response.

---

*'O most merciful redeemer, friend and brother, of you three things I pray:
to see you more clearly, love you more dearly, follow you more nearly,
day by day' (Richard of Chichester, 1197–1253).*

STEVE AISTHORPE

His master's voice

'Very truly, I tell you, anyone who does not enter the sheepfold by the gate but climbs in by another way is a thief and a bandit. The one who enters by the gate is the shepherd of the sheep. The gatekeeper opens the gate for him, and the sheep hear his voice. He calls his own sheep by name and leads them out. When he has brought out all his own, he goes ahead of them, and the sheep follow him because they know his voice.'

A popular tourist attraction in my area is a demonstration of working sheep dogs. People are mesmerised by the intimate relationship between the shepherd and his canine colleagues. The dogs' attention to his voice is absolute. Their obedience is total. But to understand Jesus' meaning in today's reading we need to set aside western ideas of farming and attempt to stand in the sandals of his hearers. These days our sheep are kept in large flocks and gathered with the aid of quad bikes and dogs. Their short lives are managed for meat production. Shepherds in first-century Palestine kept small flocks, harvesting their wool over several years. They led their sheep, calling them to follow, taking them to fresh pasture or water.

The 'sheepfold' that Jesus invites us to imagine was a communal enclosure, where different flocks would be placed for safekeeping overnight. In the morning shepherds would call their own sheep and lead them out to the day's nourishment. Jesus draws a sharp distinction between the legitimate leaders and a robber. One is forced to come in darkness and scale the wall, the other is welcomed by the gatekeeper. The call of their authentic leader resonated instantly with his flock. The sheep knew that responding to that bidding brought sustenance and safety.

After all the debating with those called to be shepherds of the people, Jesus summoned his listeners to consider who carried the hallmarks of legitimacy and who bore the signs of falsehood. The recent instance of the man born blind provided a stark example. At the hands of the Pharisees he was neglected, interrogated and expelled from fellowship. In contrast, Jesus cared, healed, sought him out and showed compassion.

Lord, so many voices compete for my attention.
Please tune my heart and mind to yours. Amen.

STEVE AISTHORPE

Superabundance and thriving

So again Jesus said to them, 'Very truly, I tell you, I am the gate for the sheep. All who came before me are thieves and bandits, but the sheep did not listen to them. I am the gate. Whoever enters by me will be saved and will come in and go out and find pasture. The thief comes only to steal and kill and destroy. I came that they may have life and have it abundantly.'

At first glance, the assertion of Jesus to be 'the gate' lacks the cosmic scope and sense of power and brilliance of a claim like 'I am the light of the world'. However, when we dig deeper, understand the context and grasp the implications of these verses, we realise this declaration is no less staggering than any of the other 'I am' statements.

The sheep enclosure we should be picturing here is a simple affair, a circular stone wall on a hillside. It is not the more substantial communal pen of the previous verses, and it has no gate. Indeed, it needs no gate because the shepherd himself would have occupied the space in the wall through which the animals would 'come in and go out'. Any potential thief or predatory animal would have to overcome the one who controlled access, in and out. It is through Jesus, the gate, that we have access to God and are 'saved' (v. 9).

The idea of having the freedom to 'come and go' may sound to us like a superficially nice idea. However, to the ears of Jesus' hearers, these words comprised a familiar phrase with a rich heritage in their scriptures. Perhaps the best-known example of its use to contemporary Christians is the evocative closing promise of Psalm 121, 'The Lord will keep your going out and your coming in from this time on and forevermore' (v. 8). It is an expression that implies the total well-being and security associated with God's blessing. It suggests a similar concept to the Hebrew word 'shalom', often translated as 'peace', but carrying a profound sense of wholeness, thriving and justice.

'So he came and proclaimed peace to you who were far off and peace to those who were near, for through him both of us have access in one Spirit to the Father' (Ephesians 2:17–18).

STEVE AISTHORPE

Good and bad shepherds

'I am the good shepherd. The good shepherd lays down his life for the sheep. The hired hand, who is not the shepherd and does not own the sheep, sees the wolf coming and leaves the sheep and runs away, and the wolf snatches them and scatters them. The hired hand runs away because a hired hand does not care for the sheep. I am the good shepherd. I know my own, and my own know me, just as the Father knows me, and I know the Father.'

In continuing to use the metaphor of sheep and shepherds to reveal himself and expose the deceitful motives of his opposers, Jesus was choosing an illustration that would not only be familiar to his hearers, but also resonate with a wealth of teaching in their scriptures. The well-known opening verse of Psalm 23, 'The Lord is my shepherd', is one of many places where God himself is portrayed as the shepherd of Israel.

When God's appointed rulers failed to lead with justice and integrity, they were branded as bad shepherds. The prophet Ezekiel characterised corrupt leaders as shepherds who fed themselves rather than the sheep and as people who failed to take care of the weak and wounded. Continuing with that metaphor, he declared that, because of the shepherds' negligence, the flock was scattered and became prey to wild animals. He then proclaimed that God would save his flock, sending a Messiah, who would be the 'good shepherd' (Ezekiel 37). Far from being a deviation from today's gospel reading, this is both the background of Jesus' choice of words and the lens through which his hearers saw his declaration to be 'the good shepherd'.

There are two Greek words that are often translated as 'good' in the New Testament. The word used by John in this fourth 'I am' statement means more than simply morally upright. It also implies that Jesus is the ideal or ultimate shepherd, and it conveys a sense of being endearing. Here then is the supreme shepherd, who truly knows his sheep and is absolutely committed to their well-being and defence.

Lord Jesus, thank you for all the ways in which you lead and feed me,
for your care and protection. Please help me to hear your voice
and follow in your ways. Amen.

STEVE AISTHORPE

Erroneous expectations?

So the Jews gathered around him and said to him, 'How long will you keep us in suspense? If you are the Messiah, tell us plainly.' Jesus answered, 'I have told you, and you do not believe. The works that I do in my Father's name testify to me, but you do not believe because you do not belong to my sheep. My sheep hear my voice. I know them, and they follow me. I give them eternal life, and they will never perish.'

As well as choosing seven miracles as 'signs' that point to Jesus' identity and seven 'I am' statements to reinforce his unveiling of the Messiah, John also mentions seven festivals. Part of God's way of shaping and encouraging his people was by giving festivals to remind them of what he had done and his promises for the future. In pinpointing the time of the encounter in today's reading, John states that it was 'the Festival of the Dedication' (10:22).

The main festivals, such as Passover, Purim and Tabernacles, corresponded to events in ancient history, but Dedication had relatively recent origins. More commonly known as Hanukkah nowadays, it celebrated the rededication of the temple after its desecration at the hands of a conquering Syrian king about two centuries earlier. After an awful chapter in Israel's history, a national hero, Judas Maccabaeus, led a revolt, liberated the people and restored the temple.

Now under Roman occupation, many people longed and hoped for a Messiah to come as a similar kind of leader and overthrow their oppressors. No wonder some were so desperate for Jesus to divulge his identity plainly. To the woman at the well in Samaria (John 4) and to the man born blind (John 9), he had already identified himself freely and clearly as 'Messiah' and 'Son of Man', so why keep these inquirers in suspense? Perhaps Jesus was unwilling to identify with the political connotations that 'Messiah' had for his exasperated questioners. Rather, he invites them to notice his actions, he longs that they will comprehend his call and follow, and he yearns for them to recognise him and receive gifts beyond their imagining.

Lord Jesus, please deliver me from any false expectations,
enable me to hear your invitation to 'come'
and receive the life you offer. Amen.

STEVE AISTHORPE

A place of significance

Then they tried to arrest him again, but he escaped from their hands. He went away again across the Jordan to the place where John had been baptising earlier, and he remained there. Many came to him, and they were saying, 'John performed no sign, but everything that John said about this man was true.' And many believed in him there.

I recently visited a village church. It was an unimpressive building. The door was open, and I slipped inside for a moment of peace and prayer. As I sat, I remembered an experience in that place 30 years ago, a moment of realisation, an encounter, that influenced decisions then and still impacts my life today.

There is much to be said for revisiting places that have been significant in our journey of faith or perhaps reconnecting with people who have been important in shaping and encouraging us. With the most challenging phase of his life approaching, Jesus returned to where his public ministry began, the scene of his baptism, where he received an affirmation that was vital to him every day since: 'This is my Son, the Beloved, with whom I am well pleased' (Matthew 3:17).

Jesus was born in 'human likeness' (Philippians 2:7), and having embraced the limitations of humanity, he faced the same challenges, temptations and choices that we do. He could allow the cries of the crowd to dictate the day's agenda or devote time to discerning God's will. He could listen to the Father in prayer or be swept along by unconsidered momentum. He knew he must 'slip away to deserted places and pray' (Luke 5:16). As long as he had work to do, Jesus continued his habit of retreating to spend time with his Father.

Those following Jesus found themselves back at the place where John first drew their attention to Jesus. At that time, it was difficult to understand. What could he mean when he said, 'He who comes after me ranks ahead of me because he was before me… the Lamb of God who takes away the sin of the world' (1:15, 29)? Now, however, they could testify that every word was true.

Is there a place or a person you might want to reconnect with?
Somewhere or someone significant in your life and faith?

STEVE AISTHORPE

Ancient wisdom for modern times: Proverbs 25—29

The book of Proverbs is a collection of wise sayings and apho- risms intended to guide people in their daily lives and into right relationship with God. Most of it, including the section we will be considering over the next two weeks, is attributed to King Solomon, who himself probably gathered some of the sayings from ancient oral tradition as well as widespread common experi- ence. While dating back as far as 700BC, Proverbs has a great deal to tell us today in our very different social context.

Though the proverbs themselves can seem random and disconnected, there are clear threads of wisdom weaving through them, perhaps the most dominant being the call to stop centring our lives on ourselves and reset our inner compass to focus on the greater good, and ultimately on God.

This message was delivered to me with some force one day by my small granddaughter. She was engrossed with her playmat with its park scene, complete with toy swings, roundabouts and benches. 'Oh, you have benches in your park,' I commented, 'so Grandma can sit down.' At this she gave me a baleful look and retorted: 'It's not all about you, Grandma.' This was perhaps forgivable because she was just repeating what her parents were frequently saying to her, in preparation for the arrival of a new sibling. However, it was also something I, and perhaps all of us, need to hear. Proverbs reminds us of this in many different ways, as we shall see.

Weaving in and out of this main theme, we are given ways of implement- ing this radical conversion in our everyday lives and recognising some of the obstacles that might undermine our best intentions. These include the problems of human arrogance, widespread injustice in the world, the general obsession with acquisition and the all-too-frequent mismatch between our prayers and our actions.

Public misconduct and personal transgression both come equally under the writer's critical gaze. Only through the grace of humility will we be ready to embrace the call to redirect the focus of our lives beyond personal advantage to the wide horizon of the needs and greater good of all creation.

MARGARET SILF

Divine arithmetic

Take away the dross from the silver, and the smith has material for a vessel; take away the wicked from the presence of the king, and his throne will be established in righteousness. Do not put yourself forward in the king's presence or stand in the place of the great, for it is better to be told, 'Come up here', than to be put lower in the presence of a noble.

Our first encounter with the upturning of our usual human assumptions and expectations comes with a reversal of standard arithmetic. All too often our normal approach to life is driven by addition or acquisition. Especially in our earlier years, our instinct is to add to our possessions, our achievements and our successes. This desire is constantly fuelled by the pressures of a consumer society to keep on acquiring more and more of things we do not need, and can ill afford.

Divine arithmetic works differently. The silver is revealed when the dross is taken away. The process is one of purification. The arithmetic is about subtraction. We are challenged to learn the art of letting go all that the Proverbs writer calls 'dross'. 'Dross' sounds very negative and, indeed, it is presented here as 'the wickedness' that stands in the way of the coming of the kingdom. It may be helpful to think of this as a challenge to be willing to let go of the superficial concerns that come between us and our true destiny as children of God. Our task in the new maths of subtraction involves learning to nourish what, in our lives, is leading us closer to God and let go of what is drawing us further away from our deepest centre. Learning to do subtraction will gradually reveal the 'silver' present deep in the heart of who we are.

This is just one aspect of the revolution that God is asking us to join. The second part of today's text calls us to stop putting our own interests first and to practise greater humility, letting go of the widespread human sense of entitlement and the assumption that we have an automatic right to the best place at the table.

When we learn to do subtraction, rights give way to responsibilities and 'I' stands humbly behind 'we'.

MARGARET SILF

The power of kindness

What your eyes have seen do not hastily bring into court, for what will you do in the end, when your neighbour puts you to shame? Argue your case with your neighbour directly, and do not disclose another's secret, or else someone who hears you will bring shame upon you, and your ill repute will have no end. A word fitly spoken is like apples of gold in a setting of silver. Like a gold ring or an ornament of gold is a wise rebuke to a listening ear.

There is a natural tendency for us to be eager to spread news, especially if we are the first to have seen an event or heard a significant conversation. Showing restraint is another aspect of the spiritual revolution to which we are being called. There is also a natural assumption that right and justice are on our side in the various conflicts that we encounter in our daily lives. It can be a hard lesson to discover that our own judgement is often severely flawed.

It follows that making quick judgements and acting on them can be dangerous. No matter how convinced we may be, the Proverbs writer warns us not to rush to litigation. Some recent high-profile court cases have shown how deeply embarrassing it can be when claims to the moral high ground are shot down in court. The situation can become toxic in a very public way if information is disclosed that, whether true or false, should have remained confidential.

We are warned that in most cases a better alternative is to have a civilised conversation with our neighbour and try to come to an informal agreement. Our differences remain private, and neither party is unnecessarily shamed. A just and positive outcome is often possible with much less acrimony. Public conflict in open court, on the other hand, rarely ends without real harm being done to all participants.

Even better: kind and generous words, we learn, are balm to the soul if offered in encouragement and support, and likely to be effective even if spoken in well-intentioned rebuke.

May I learn to be kind, and if I cannot be kind,
may I have the grace to be quiet.

MARGARET SILF

The sun and the north wind

With patience a ruler may be persuaded, and a soft tongue can break bones… If your enemies are hungry, give them bread to eat, and if they are thirsty, give them water to drink, for you will heap coals of fire on their heads, and the Lord will reward you. The north wind produces rain, and a backbiting tongue, angry looks.

There is a story about a contest between the sun and the north wind. Seeing a person who was taking a walk dressed in a warm overcoat, the wind said to the sun, 'Just watch me, I can make that walker down there take off his coat.' And with this, the north wind blew and blew and blew, but all that the wind achieved was to make the walker draw his coat even more tightly around himself. 'What you are doing will never succeed,' smiled the sun. 'Now just watch me instead.' And the sun shone down warmly on the walker, who, soon enough, took off his coat spontaneously.

The writer of Proverbs speaks here, metaphorically, of the north wind as a bringer of negativity and spite. By contrast, he urges us to use gentleness, generosity and kindness when engaging with others. He reminds us that by doing this we are 'heaping coals of fire' on the other's head. This might sound more like a form of medieval torture, but more probably here it carries the meaning of leading the other person towards repentance and renewal, rather than inflicting punishment.

This is an example of the recurring theme in Proverbs of how discipline motivated by kindness is more effective in drawing others towards a better way of life than either vindictive punishment or insincere flattery would be. This applies as much to our relationships in the family as to our wider social interactions. Prefiguring the gospel, the writer urges us to give food and drink to those who need it, to treat others as we would wish to be treated ourselves. As in the old story, the sun works more effectively than the north wind to bring about a change of heart.

Just as the gentle rain can dissolve the hardest rock,
so kindness has far more power than force.

MARGARET SILF

The delusion of self-satisfaction

Do you see people wise in their own eyes? There is more hope for fools than for them. The lazy person says, 'There is a lion in the road! There is a lion in the streets!' As a door turns on its hinge, so does a lazy person in bed. The lazy person buries a hand in the dish and is too tired to bring it back to the mouth. The lazy person is wiser in self-esteem than seven who can answer discreetly.

As an excuse for failing to fulfil what is required or expected, 'There's a lion in the streets' comes close to 'The dog ate my homework'. The chances of there being lions roaming the local township are even lower than the misbehaviour of the family pet – although the dog of an acquaintance of mine recently really did chew up her passport just before she was due to depart the country!

An appealing aspect of the writer's style is his creative use of language and figures of speech. The comparison of a lazy person turning over in bed for another snooze to a door turning on its hinges, perhaps with accompanying squeaking and grunting, or, having reached for food, being too idle to lift it to his mouth, are good examples of his skill as a wordsmith. This skill imprints these images on our minds, so that they have far greater impact than less expressive language could have achieved.

Following on from these playful metaphors we come to a simple, yet astonishing statement – that the lazy person, for all his manifest faults, is 'wiser in self-esteem' (v. 16) than the person who has a more orderly lifestyle. Being 'wiser in self-esteem', in this context, is a polite way of describing those who have a high opinion of themselves. And this is precisely the warning being given here. When we think we are wise, accomplished and sophisticated, we are deluding ourselves. This delusion is at the root of our need for radical change. Only when we realise how little we really know or understand can God begin the necessary work of purification in our hearts.

May our eyes be opened to recognise our true limitations,
so that with awakened hearts we become open to
the transforming power of grace.

MARGARET SILF

Feeding what leads to life

For lack of wood the fire goes out, and where there is no whisperer, quarrelling ceases. As charcoal is to hot embers and wood to fire, so is a quarrelsome person for kindling strife. The words of a whisperer are like delicious morsels; they go down into the inner parts of the body. Like the glaze covering an earthen vessel are smooth lips with an evil heart.

Some of the most notorious turning points in human history began with a single spark of anger. Devastating wars have been triggered by a single shot. Today's reading confronts us with another human tendency: to assume that there is nothing much we can do to influence the course of history, either for good or ill.

The powerful message for today is that fire only burns when it is fuelled. If there is no fuel, there will be no fire. Yet we rarely see ourselves as contributing to that fuel supply. Today we are reminded that if we all refuse to add the fuel of angry thoughts and words to the fires that threaten peace on earth, there will be no conflict. We feed the flames of conflict not only when we quarrel with others, but also when we give our energy and attention, and sometimes even our approval, to the contentious content in our press and social media.

Peace and conflict are, respectively, like plants and weeds in the garden. The ones we feed, by giving them our energy and attention, will grow. The ones we starve, or even dig out, will shrink and die. Which do we want to nourish: the plants or the weeds, the peace or the conflict?

The writer suggests that the spread of negativity also has a secret, stealthy nature, seeping into our hearts and minds like a slow poison, often hidden behind fake smiles and smooth talking. We know that when dark secrets are whispered and we are asked not to divulge them, something is wrong. We are not as helpless as we think. It is in our power to add fuel to the flames of strife or to kindle the warmth of peace and harmony. It's a choice we make many times every day.

Conflict spreads like wildfire. May we keep on choosing peace.

MARGARET SILF

The boomerang effect

Whoever digs a pit will fall into it, and a stone will come back on the one who starts it rolling. A lying tongue hates its victims, and a flattering mouth works ruin. Do not boast about tomorrow, for you do not know what a day may bring. Let another praise you and not your own mouth, a stranger and not your own lips... Better is open rebuke than hidden love. Well meant are the wounds a friend inflicts, but profuse are the kisses of an enemy.

Today's reading warns of the boomerang effect of our actions. I once accidentally reversed my car into a half-finished inspection pit in a friend's garden. The kind of pit referred to in today's reading, however, is a deliberate pit, dug intentionally to trap a victim. It is the product of an evil purpose.

The boomerang used by indigenous peoples in Australia is likewise designed not for malicious ends but to return to its owner once it has accomplished its task of hunting for food. The stones in the reading are the kind of missile aimed deliberately at a victim in order to kill or maim.

In the case of both the pit and the stones, the intention is malevolent, and when this is so the writer warns us that the digger of the pit and the thrower of the stone will themselves fall victim to their own evil purposes. Today we might call this the law of unintended consequences. When we wish harm on another, harm will come back upon ourselves or others.

Most of us are unlikely to dig pits or throw stones, but we may try to trap people in other ways, perhaps by deliberately misleading them, confusing them with our arguments or tricking them into saying or doing something they regret. Jesus had to deal with this kind of trap several times. Stones also come in many forms, from the barbed remark uttered to hurt another to the malicious rumour that can derail another's life.

The writer warns against all forms of deception, repeating the warning to beware of false praise, especially when we praise ourselves, but to remain open to honest criticism.

We all live in glass houses.
The stones we throw cause more damage than we expect.

MARGARET SILF

Homing instinct

Like a bird that strays from its nest is one who strays from home. Perfume and incense make the heart glad, but the soul is torn by trouble. Do not forsake your friend or the friend of your parent; do not go to the house of your kindred on the day of your calamity. Better is a neighbour who is nearby than kindred who are far away. Be wise, my child, and make my heart glad, so that I may answer whoever reproaches me.

The miracle of homing is all around us. After years in the open ocean, fish return to the river where they first hatched. Birds and butterflies make seasonal migratory journeys of thousands of miles to arrive at the place they recognise as home. Newly hatched turtles follow the light of the moon as they struggle to find their way to the sea. We human beings also often long to return to our roots or our families as we grow older, and many at the end of their lives wish to die at home, close to those they love.

The pull of home is a survival instinct. As today's reading reminds us, to stray from the nest, the place of nurture and safety, is dangerous. We can be seduced by the delights of 'perfume and incense', the superficial attractions that the world offers, but deep down, to stray from our true home is to invite pain and trouble.

St Augustine declared to God: 'My soul is restless until it finds its rest in you.' Our hearts, likewise, find no rest until we find our way home, to that deepest centre of ourselves, where God is indwelling – the God who is closer to us than our own next breath.

The German language describes our experience of home in human terms as '*die kleine heile Welt*' – that small but wholesome world of friends, family and community where we know we belong and where we are grounded and held, especially through the extreme turbulence we are experiencing in our times. The strength of this circle depends on each of us being faithful to it, not forsaking it in pursuit of transient pleasures.

Home is where the heart is; God's heart is where our home is.

MARGARET SILF

Interdependence

Anyone who tends a fig tree will eat its fruit, and anyone who takes care of a master will be honoured. Just as water reflects the face, so one human heart reflects another. Sheol and Abaddon are never satisfied, and human eyes are never satisfied. The crucible is for silver, and the furnace is for gold, so a person is tested by being praised. Crush a fool in a mortar with a pestle along with crushed grain, but the folly will not be driven out.

There is a French parable: the sun decides one day not to shine because it sheds its light to ripen the crops but gets nothing in return. The rain stops falling because the earth gives nothing in return. The earth feels exploited and stops nourishing the grain, and the grain, which gives its life to make bread for humankind refuses to germinate because it gets nothing in return, and so it comes to pass that life dies out on earth.

Today's reading tells a similar story: if you tend the fig tree, it will bear fruit to nourish you. By implication, if you refuse to tend the fig, it will not bear fruit. The same applies to our relationships with others. If we take care of each other, care will be taken of us. Long-term, committed faithful service is the way to honour this interdependence.

Next we are reminded that the true nature of another lies in the depths of that person's heart. Our physical image is reflected back to us by still waters, but our soul is revealed only through the lens of the heart. However, this comes with a stark warning: Sheol and Abaddon (Death and Destruction) are insatiable, just like the insatiable human desire for more and more.

This compulsion for unbridled acquisition obscures the lens of the heart and blinds us to our true selves and the true selves of others. Only the divine refining process can sift the gold and silver from the dross, clear the vision of the heart and free us from the deadly grip of death and destruction.

When we look at our image in the mirror may we learn to see
there the image of all our sisters and brothers reflected back to us.

MARGARET SILF

Caretakers of creation

Know well the condition of your flocks, and give attention to your herds, for riches do not last forever, nor a crown for all generations. When the grass is gone, and new growth appears, and the herbage of the mountains is gathered, the lambs will provide your clothing, and the goats the price of a field; there will be enough goats' milk for your food, for the food of your household, and nourishment for your female servants.

My cousin would have fully appreciated today's reading. A sheep farmer in Lincolnshire, he had finally managed to get to bed one night after an exhausting day caring for his flock at lambing time. Perhaps as he began to drift off into much-needed sleep, he was thinking of those ewes who were due to give birth and would soon need his help. But his dreaming was abruptly interrupted by a peal of thunder as a fierce storm broke out overhead.

He did not hesitate and was instantly out of bed and down to the lambing shed, where he spent the night caring for the condition of his flock. When he finally got back home hours later, he found that a nearby tree had been struck by lightning, bringing down a heavy branch through the roof of his bedroom and crashing straight across his bed.

This is a story of priorities and responsibilities. We are caretakers of creation, and our first task is to know and look after that particular part of creation entrusted to our care: our children, our elders, our pets, our flocks, our fields and gardens, our neighbours and all the life that shares our patch of earth. Life, as my cousin discovered, is fragile, and the riches we think we have can disappear in a flash.

Yet life continues; more lambs will be born, and fresh grass will grow. The goats will thrive and give us milk, cheese and the price of a new field. The life we nurture will nurture us in the great interdependent circle of life, continuing to provide for us, if we continue to provide for them. Are we willing to embrace our part in this sacred contract?

Creation faithfully, generously and selflessly cares for us.
A faithful, generous and unselfish response is asked of us.

MARGARET SILF

Quiet thoughtfulness

When a land rebels it has many rulers; but with an intelligent person, honesty endures. A poor person who oppresses the poor is a beating rain that leaves no food. Those who forsake the law praise the wicked, but those who keep the law struggle against them. The evil do not understand justice, but those who seek the Lord understand it completely. Better to be poor and walk in integrity than to be crooked in one's ways even though rich.

I was once the reluctant witness of something approaching a stampede in the centre of a big city. A football match had just ended and hundreds of fans, fuelled by disappointment or triumph respectively, surged through the main shopping street in a terrifying anarchic mass. Most people took cover in the shop entrances, but one old lady was caught in the rush. We watched in horror as she took one of the rioters by the shoulders and spoke to him. Whatever she said, this youngster turned to jelly and began to shake. It was a startling example of how the calm confrontation of one thoughtful person can be more powerful than the unruly chaos of the mob.

Authoritarian regimes often adopt the policy of 'divide and rule' to maintain control over their populations. Today's reading warns us that this is not the sign of intelligent government, where unity is valued over division and order over chaos. It takes courage to struggle against the force of the mob, just as the lady in the story challenged the young man who was being swept away in the fury of the crowd. It takes courage to uphold the law in the face of mass lawlessness.

It takes even more courage to stand up for truth and justice in a totalitarian regime, where this may bring you and your family face to face with the threat of torture and death. Many brave individuals, struggling in such regimes, have lost everything for the sake of integrity and have tested for themselves the truth of today's message, that it is better to be honestly impoverished than dishonestly enriched.

When the storm breaks, may we have the courage to choose truth over comfort and safety, and integrity over easy gain.

MARGARET SILF

When prayer and action do not match

When one will not listen to the law, even one's prayers are an abomination. Those who mislead the upright into evil ways will fall into pits of their own making, but the blameless will have a goodly inheritance. The rich is wise in self-esteem, but an intelligent poor person sees through the pose. When the righteous rejoice, there is great glory, but when the wicked prevail, people go into hiding.

What happens when our actions do not match our prayers? I guess this question has troubled most of us at some point over the course of our lives. Today's reading introduces us to those who flout the law but still expect their prayers to be heard. These prayers, the writer tells us, are an abomination, loathsome to God. Jesus was less extreme in his censure, but nevertheless urges us always to let our prayers be compatible with our actions.

The writer reserves even fiercer condemnation for those who wilfully mislead others into choosing a wrong course and warns that they will come to a bad end. Jesus likewise vehemently condemns the hypocrites who hide their wickedness beneath a veneer of feigned righteousness. These are the ones who have a high opinion of themselves, which he sarcastically expresses as 'wise in self-esteem'. He reassures us, however, that an intelligent person, however poor, will see through the counterfeit promises of the liars and deceivers.

It does not always work out quite like that, though, as we know to our cost. Whole populations can be deceived by propaganda that has its own hidden agendas. When this deception succeeds, people go into hiding, afraid to speak their truth in the face of opposition and retribution. When goodness and truth prevail, however, life can be lived to the full and something of the glory of God is revealed.

How might we contribute to the reign of goodness on earth? We begin, Proverbs suggests, by examining our lives and becoming sensitive to those times when the actions and choices of our lives fail to match the prayers of our hearts.

Actions that do not match our prayers are like pieces of a jigsaw that do not fit but have to be forced into place. They spoil the whole picture.

MARGARET SILF

True authority

Like a roaring lion or a charging bear is a wicked ruler over a poor people. A ruler who lacks understanding is a cruel oppressor, but one who hates unjust gain will enjoy a long life… One who walks in integrity will be safe, but whoever follows crooked ways will fall into the Pit. Anyone who tills the land will have plenty of bread, but one who follows worthless pursuits will have plenty of poverty. The faithful will abound with blessings, but one who is in a hurry to be rich will not go unpunished.

There seems to be no shortage of roaring lions and charging bears holding high office in the world today. We hear from them daily and feel the force of their charging. What wisdom does Proverbs offer with regard to these power-wielders?

There is a clue in the word 'understanding'. What is not being understood by the lions and the bears is the nature of power. In *Measure for Measure*, Shakespeare, speaking of 'man, proud man, dressed in a little brief authority, most ignorant of what he's most assured', accurately describes such rulers. The authority they wield is brief and superficial. They believe themselves to be all-powerful, yet they lack any understanding of the people they control. The power they exert is 'power over' their people, the power to impose their own will on others.

This is the opposite of the power of the Holy Spirit, who works quite differently, empowering us from within, awakening courage, strength and wisdom that we did not know we possessed. The power of the tyrant oppresses; the power of God liberates. The power of the tyrant sends in the tanks; the power of God changes minds and hearts.

It is, however, all too easy to overlook our own shortcomings by focusing on these external oppressors. There may be a (less noisily) roaring lion and a (less energetically) charging bear active in ourselves. There is little we can do about ego-driven rulers, apart from the route of the ballot box, but we can, and must, acknowledge and address any signs of these traits in our own behaviour.

The only true authority granted to humankind
flows from the author of creation, never from ourselves.

MARGARET SILF

Energy theft

Scoffers set a city aflame, but the wise turn away wrath. If the wise go to law with fools, there is ranting and ridicule without relief. The blood-thirsty hate the blameless, and they seek the life of the upright. A fool gives full vent to anger, but the wise quietly holds it back. If a ruler listens to falsehood, all his officials will be wicked.

No one loves a scoffer. Proverbs warns us that scoffers set the city on fire, and it is certainly true that the voice of a scoffer will sell more newspapers or attract more followers on social media than a more reasoned, moderate voice would do. Scoffers appeal to the worst in us and stir up resentments and jealousies that would be better left buried.

Scoffing is a way of expressing contempt for another person, by jeering at them or pouring scorn on their lives or achievements. By any standard it is unpleasant and damaging behaviour. Its potential for harm is deep-rooted, because it is a classic form of energy theft. Most of us would not go round to our neighbour's drive and syphon fuel out of their car. But how easy it is to steal each other's emotional and spiritual energy in other, less obvious, ways. Scoffing is one of those ways.

The balance of our inner energy is a bit like a see-saw. Some things leave us feeling 'up', others 'down'. For example, when someone says something kind or positive, it raises our spirits a little. Destructive criticism, on the other hand, can leave us feeling low. It is a sad fact that the scoffer gets a brief 'high' from putting the other person down. We all know people who seem to light up the room when they come in, and others who seem to suck the energy out of it. Sustained exposure to someone who drains our energy can be seriously damaging.

The reading equates scoffers with fools and repeats the warning that we will recognise them by their tendency to bluster, lie and have angry outbursts, while the wise quietly stand their ground with restraint.

The final warning in today's passage rings true in today's world: a foolish ruler will surround himself with foolish 'advisers'.

The waters of wisdom run deep and calm.

MARGARET SILF

A radical revolution

A person's pride will bring humiliation, but one who is lowly in spirit will obtain honour. To be a partner of a thief is to hate one's own life; one hears the victim's curse but discloses nothing. The fear of others lays a snare, but one who trusts in the Lord is secure. Many seek the favour of a ruler, but it is from the Lord that one gets justice. The unjust are an abomination to the righteous, but the upright are an abomination to the wicked.

On this final day of our journey with this section of Proverbs, we are confronted again by the writer's repeated, and obviously heartfelt, reminder that the dynamic of grace turns all our assumptions and expectations on their heads. Pride will ultimately lead to humiliation, but humility will yield to honour of a far greater quality. Fear can dominate our human lives, but what is truly important is trust. Injustice is all around us, but justice is the characteristic of God's reign. The wicked, the unjust and the fools are placed next to the wise, the just and the righteous and will ultimately always be found wanting. This has been the message that weaves through all these chapters of Proverbs.

How will this overturning of values happen? A radical change is called for. We call this conversion or 'metanoia', and it involves a complete reversal of our habitual human ways of proceeding. It may need to happen over and over again, every day. The truth is that we usually think of events in terms of how they affect us. There is a universal temptation to put ourselves, our tribe, our country centre stage and expect the rest of the world to revolve around us. The wisdom of Proverbs, and indeed the challenge of the gospel, requires us to centre our lives not on our own ego but on the deeper needs of all life.

When this happens, the world begins to tilt on its axis: humility is valued more highly than pride, trust more highly than fear, wisdom more highly than foolishness, justice more highly than wrongdoing and the greater good more highly than personal advantage.

Every choice will either further this radical transformation or impede it. It matters how we choose.

MARGARET SILF

The letter to the Galatians

No one disputes that the letter to the Galatians comes from the apostle Paul and was one of the earliest he wrote, probably between AD40 and 50. He has had an association with this church (or churches) for some time, having established them earlier, but he now finds himself needing to defend himself and his message. At times he is scathing of the ease with which the Galatian Christians have departed from the message he brought them. At other times, he pleads in a maternal way and to their former relationship as the basis for a renewed association.

There is a problem at the heart of Paul's letter: those who had responded to his preaching have now overlaid his message with practices brought to them by others initially outside the fellowship. Paul is outraged, because this creates a distortion of the good news. Carefully but forcefully, Paul shows that Jesus is the great promise of God, whose coming was always foretold in the scriptures. Jesus is no 'afterthought' when things have finally become so serious God needs a Plan B!

And this means our response is on the basis of God's own promise and gracious invitation. We cannot retain or assume any set of laws or customs to guarantee this offer of life. In the words of the apostle himself, we 'know that a person is not justified by the works of the law, but by faith in Jesus Christ. So we, too, have put our faith in Christ Jesus that we may be justified by faith in Christ and not by the works of the law, because by the works of the law no one will be justified' (Galatians 2:16, NIV).

This confident assertion allows Paul to explain his understanding of the law and also the work of the Holy Spirit. The law was given because it shows us that we are sinful. However, once we have been justified, we remain faithful to God by the power and inspiration of the Holy Spirit. Again, the law cannot compel this good life. It is only possible with God's help.

Our readings will track Paul's arguments and appeals but also come to us as a fresh invitation to find our hope in God alone and to trust his power to lead us forward as disciples of Jesus Christ.

ANDY JOHN

It's about Jesus

Grace to you and peace from God our Father and the Lord Jesus Christ, who gave himself for our sins to set us free from the present evil age, according to the will of our God and Father, to whom be the glory forever and ever. Amen. I am astonished that you are so quickly deserting the one who called you.

At the heart of the Christian story stands the person of Jesus Christ. The first Christians encountered the saving and transforming love of God in a unique way in Jesus' life and ministry and then supremely in his death and resurrection. As they reflected on and grew in their faith, nurtured by the Holy Spirit, they came to see that Jesus stood at the very heart of God's plans for humanity and the whole universe. In the words of Paul: 'In him all things in heaven and on earth were created, things visible and invisible, whether thrones or dominions or rulers or powers – all things have been created through him and for him' (Colossians 1:16).

This is the good news which Paul announces at the outset of his letter. It is a triumphant declaration that the greatest shift in human destiny has occurred because Jesus has given himself for our sins. He has opened the future to us as well as resolving our broken past. We might, in the light of this, expect a confident invitation to continue in the grace offered to us, but something has gone terribly wrong in the lives of the Galatian Christians. Having started with God, they have deserted him. As we shall discover, a journey might begin well but it will require constant nurture and can easily become distorted. We can find ourselves lost once more and separated from God, because our choices have been poor.

The invitation from our reading today takes us to the centre and heart of our faith but with an urgent appeal not to depart from the truth however well our journey may have started.

Lord Jesus Christ, you gave yourself for us so that we might become followers. Lead us so that we might not depart, but walk with you ever more closely. Amen.

ANDY JOHN

It's about Paul too

But when the one who had set me apart before I was born and called me through his grace was pleased to reveal his Son to me, so that I might proclaim him among the gentiles, I did not confer with any human, nor did I go up to Jerusalem to those who were already apostles before me, but I went away at once into Arabia, and afterwards I returned to Damascus.

Having set out the heart of the good news and challenged the Galatian Christians about departing from the gospel, Paul begins to outline his credentials. He has already told them that this gospel was not humanly crafted but came directly from God. He now places the divine origin of his message in all eternity. More than this: God's purposes, he asserts, have been from the beginning. Like Jeremiah, who was called even before he was in the womb (Jeremiah 1:5), Paul understands that God has foreordained him – that is, planned ahead the way his life will now be committed to the Gentiles. His unwavering confidence in this revelation was such that he found no need to consult immediately with the first Christian leaders in Jerusalem. More than this, perhaps, there could be no possibility the message could be tainted by human intervention.

We can begin to understand the sort of challenge Paul was facing and why he writes like this. First, he needs to establish that his message is from God and therefore beyond any doubt or dispute. It needs no authentication from anyone else, including the first apostles. Second, if this message is from God, it means that Paul can speak with authority. We will read how he takes issue with some who doubt his intentions as well as his credibility as an apostle. The message and the man therefore stand together as the guarantee and ground of faith. In essence, he is challenging the Galatian Christians to hold to this message, to return if they have departed and to believe, without any doubt, the news they once held dear.

We give you thanks, heavenly Father, for the care you have taken in revealing your Son, Jesus Christ. May we share Paul's confidence that this is your chosen message for the world today. Amen.

ANDY JOHN

Checking in

But because of false brothers and sisters… who slipped in to spy on the freedom we have in Christ Jesus, so that they might enslave us – we did not submit to them even for a moment… When James and Cephas and John… recognised the grace that had been given to me, they gave to Barnabas and me the right hand of fellowship, agreeing that we should go to the gentiles… They asked only one thing, that we remember the poor, which was actually what I was eager to do.

In our reading today, Paul begins to clarify where the threat to the Galatians lay. Some had joined the company of believers but were insisting on certain beliefs and practices to supplement their fledgling faith. He describes them as false believers because their practices were so far removed from Paul's message that he could not recognise them as legitimate believers. The level of change to his message had so distorted the gospel that it could not be regarded as the truth.

The influence of some who insisted new converts adopt practices from the law became a source of conflict throughout Paul's ministry. His insistence this was not necessary was based on a clear principle that we are brought to God through Jesus and made one with him through faith. Our life in Christ is sustained not by remedies which provide a tight framework for faithfulness but on our dependence on the Holy Spirit.

Paul's vocation, affirmed by the Jerusalem leaders, was that he should take this gospel to the Gentiles with one emphasis, that of caring for the poor. We can therefore see the nature of Paul's gospel. It is the 'spiritual', dynamic grace of God which breaks through human sin, claiming us for a life of faithful following. At the same time it is the 'material', grounded good news which compels us to serve and to work for justice for those most in need. This is a powerful message which still defines the task for the church across the world, and it is this to which we are all called.

Faithful God, as we thank you for the good news,
we pray for grace to inhabit your truth each day
for Jesus Christ's sake. Amen.

ANDY JOHN

Pressure points

But when Cephas came to Antioch, I opposed him to his face, because he stood self-condemned, for until certain people came from James, he used to eat with the gentiles. But after they came, he drew back and kept himself separate for fear of the circumcision faction. And the other Jews joined him in this hypocrisy, so that even Barnabas was led astray by their hypocrisy.

Paul's attack on those who insisted on the inclusion of extra rituals to be fully included in the church might seem strange to us today. In today's reading, however, we can see its effects and how group dynamics present powerful challenges. Prior to the entrance of those who claimed the law was necessary to effect full obedience to God, Peter had associated with the Gentiles. But now, both afraid of their censure and perhaps in order to be seen to maintain a form of purity, he withdraws from them.

And here we see the problem. This undermines what Paul knows to be the heart of the gospel. God has chosen us in Christ, freely and on the basis of his own promises rather than on a legal framework. The inclusion of all is on the basis of grace revealed in Jesus. We are held within this grace by God's life-giving Spirit and not by following a code.

But the group dynamic can be all but irresistible. Peter and later Barnabas succumb, and their distance from the Gentile believers reasserts something abolished by the cross. We can understand Paul confronting the older apostle. What was at stake was not only an unacceptable separation into two groups of the one church but a dismantling of the gospel itself. We might understand the kind of pressures Peter and Barnabas faced but it is worth remembering Jesus calls people to take up a cross and to deny themselves. This can be costly but without it there can be no true freedom and no authentic grace.

Heavenly Father, your Son calls us into fellowship with you.
Keep us resolute in the grace by which you have called us,
for his sake. Amen.

ANDY JOHN

Justified and living in Christ

For through the law I died to the law, so that I might live to God. I have been crucified with Christ, and it is no longer I who live, but it is Christ who lives in me. And the life I now live in the flesh I live by faith in the Son of God, who loved me and gave himself for me. I do not nullify the grace of God, for if righteousness comes through the law, then Christ died for nothing.

In our reading today, we encounter the heart of the gospel. But it comes with a kind of health warning. Paul has confronted the Galatians about their direction of travel. They are moving away, departing from the good news he brought them. His contention, especially in view of those who were demanding they observe certain customs and laws, is that there is now only one ground for faith: it is Jesus and his saving death. Our faith in him has united us to his death and resurrection, which has brought an end to the law and any need to make it the point of entry into a relationship with God.

His astonishing claim is that uniting with Christ is so profound that our former lives of separation and sin come to an abrupt end. In the language recorded by John, we are 'born again' (John 3:3) and a life sustained by the Holy Spirit enables us to live no longer as strangers to God, but rather as friends and, extraordinarily, as children of our heavenly Father (Romans 8:15).

For us today this offers both invitation and challenge: there is only one thing which is all-important and that is our relationship to Jesus Christ. This, and only this, is the ground of our faith. And so it is here that we have supreme confidence. Our destiny has been secured by him and his once-for-all sacrifice. In the words of a beautiful hymn: 'Here is love vast as the ocean, loving kindness as the flood.'

Lord Jesus, Saviour and friend, I thank you for your life laid down.
You have set me free to know you and follow you. Amen.

ANDY JOHN

The promise of the Spirit

The only thing I want to learn from you is this: Did you receive the Spirit by doing the works of the law or by believing what you heard? Are you so foolish? Having started with the Spirit, are you now ending with the flesh? Did you experience so much for nothing? – if it really was for nothing. Well then, does God supply you with the Spirit and work miracles among you by your doing the works of the law or by your believing what you heard?

The Covid-19 pandemic gave us new words and practices. We became accustomed to speaking about the 'new normal' and how life might be forever different. Today that phrase is redeemed as we are offered a different 'new normal' and all that it promises the sons and daughters of God.

We can hear some of the anger and energy in Paul's words, and with good reason, as Paul insists that there is no need for the Galatians to return to things from which they have been released. If the ground of our faith is that Jesus has died to unite us to him, the proof of this is revealed by our life in the Spirit. The gift of the Holy Spirit is evidence that we are God's own on the basis of what Christ offers in his death and resurrection.

It is easy to miss the vitality of what Paul is also saying here. It is by the Spirit of God that a life of grace and power is ours. The gift of the Spirit is not only a proof, therefore; it is the very life of God which sustains us for our life in Christ. This is the fulness promised by Jesus (John 10:10) and the 'new normal' for Christian people everywhere. To us, removed from arguments about laws and rituals, the invitation comes with new force: will we allow the Holy Spirit of God to bring the life of the kingdom to us, flowing in and out in new acts of love and service?

---

*Lord, send your Spirit to empower us as we have come to you
in and through your death and resurrection. Amen.*

ANDY JOHN

A law leading where?

My point is this: the law, which came four hundred thirty years later, does not annul a covenant previously ratified by God, so as to nullify the promise. For if the inheritance comes from the law, it no longer comes from the promise, but God granted it to Abraham through the promise. Why then the law? It was added because of transgressions, until the offspring would come to whom the promise had been made.

In this next section, we see Paul the former rabbi using a style of argument which was used frequently but which we haven't seen before. Nonetheless, he is not deviating from his central argument one bit: he has insisted that the ground of faith is the redeeming work of Jesus Christ. It is by his death that we are restored to God and we access this grace by faith alone.

There is a way of stating this which suggests his coming was late in the day or, to caricature a little, an afterthought. The argument would run like this: 'God sent Jesus because everything else had failed and this would finally resolve the human tendency to sin when other measures had failed.' And of course, this is quite wrong! Paul now makes it clear that Jesus is the first great promise and his coming is the fulfilment of what God always purposed. The law was never intended to supplant God's promise given to Abraham nor to change the ground of salvation. The law was added because of sin. The law reveals and surfaces what is true: that we are all sinners in need of grace.

In other words, it is the faithful and consistent purposes of God which Paul is commending here. Jesus is the fulfilment of God's promise. We have come to share in this inheritance because of Jesus alone. Our reading today therefore helps us place the cross and resurrection in the context of God's sovereignty which will not be defeated. And because of this, we have hope.

Heavenly Father, your purposes have not failed
and you have made it possible for us to know you
through Jesus Christ. We give you our deepest thanks. Amen.

ANDY JOHN

One in Christ

But now that faith has come, we are no longer subject to a disciplinarian, for in Christ Jesus you are all children of God through faith. As many of you as were baptised into Christ have clothed yourselves with Christ. There is no longer Jew or Greek; there is no longer slave or free; there is no longer male and female, for all of you are one in Christ Jesus. And if you belong to Christ, then you are Abraham's offspring, heirs according to the promise.

As the youngest child in my family, I was used to receiving the hand-me-downs from my older brother. Shirts and trousers would regularly come my way once he had grown out of them, if they were still in good condition. Sometimes their condition was not the issue; it was whether they fit. Wearing baggy trousers was social death!

In our reading for today, Paul unpacks one of those ideas which has become central to our thinking about the radical nature of the gospel. In an age where social distinction, rank and status was supremely important, Paul tells us there is an absolute equality for all Christians. We are all, he writes 'one in Christ'. We can see how this is the inevitable outcome of his earlier arguments that the basis of faith is not the law but only Jesus. Regardless of background or anything else, we come to God only at his invitation, but the invitation is wonderfully made to each of us. Kings and princes have no greater access than anyone else to the halls of the great king!

As with the garments I received from my brother, the challenge is for each of us to inhabit this new identity well. Paul tells us we have been clothed with Christ. To wear these clothes well means embracing the appearance of Jesus – doing the same things he did and becoming like him in our inner (and outer) being. How can we allow him to shape us such that our words, thoughts and deeds reflect him increasingly?

Living God, mould us in the image of Jesus and reflect through us his own beauty and holiness, for he is your Son and our Lord. Amen.

ANDY JOHN

Divine exchange

But when the fullness of time had come, God sent his Son, born of a woman, born under the law, in order to redeem those who were under the law, so that we might receive adoption as children. And because you are children, God has sent the Spirit of his Son into our hearts, crying, 'Abba! Father!' So you are no longer a slave but a child, and if a child then also an heir through God.

In our previous reading we understood our status as Christians was due to the death and resurrection of Jesus. This is the point of entry for each of us without distinction. Inhabiting this identity is one of the blessings and challenges we face. In today's passage, Paul expands this idea and shows how the promise given to Jesus comes to us because we are united with him. Since we have been baptised into him, we are received as children by adoption and, like Jesus, can name God as our Father.

It is worth exploring this idea because it faces several challenges.

First, it is sometimes thought that the title 'Abba' can infantilise. In other words, we adopt childish thinking and are not able to think or question intelligently. However, it is worth recalling that Paul urges mindful maturity (Colossians 1:28) and understood how important it was to grasp the truth of what God has revealed in Jesus.

Second, there will be some for whom associations with a father has been negative and the idea that God could be like an earthly father is distressing. I have come to believe that Paul's emphasis that we inherit the blessings of Christ is a helpful way of approaching this matter. We stand in a relationship with God whose love is beyond compare and shoulder to shoulder with Jesus. Many will find the only appropriate way of understanding this is to exclaim 'Abba! Father!', but for each of us it is the mercy and grace received which will suffice. God knows our hearts and minds and is able to hold us all in his love.

Lord Jesus Christ, Saviour and friend, we rejoice that
we have inherited blessings beyond our understanding.
Teach us to know your God and ours, our heavenly Father. Amen.

ANDY JOHN

Love which pleads

Brothers and sisters, I beg you: become as I am, for I also have become as you are. You have done me no wrong. You know that it was because of a physical infirmity that I first announced the gospel to you; though my condition put you to the test, you did not scorn or despise me but welcomed me as an angel of God, as Christ Jesus. What has become of the goodwill you felt? For I testify that, had it been possible, you would have torn out your eyes and given them to me.

In today's passage, there is a significant change in Paul's writing which opens questions about pastoral care and conflict: two vital questions in the church! We see him altering the nature of his appeal, which becomes more personal and gentle. He is clearly deeply worried that their journey of faith is now leading them away from Christ and the good news. Here he no longer refers to scripture or logic but rather to the heart.

We also ought to note that pastoral care is therefore not a question of being 'nice'. Paul's concern is real and urgent. Later he will become more animated and suggest a course of drastic action (Galatians 5:12)! But on occasions bare logic and the claim to facts can prove quite fruitless. Paul references his own weakness or infirmity (v. 13) and their former love for him. I have made the mistake, on many occasions, of trying to win an argument when an appeal to the heart would have been not only appropriate but also more effective.

Secondly, he is reconnecting their relationship. In other words, he is revisiting a place of mutual trust which was once vital to them all. Finding common ground and language is one of the most important and respectful ways of dismantling conflict and discerning ways of listening and understanding. Paul will return to his logic, but by reminding the Galatians of their once precious trust, he is underlining his sincerity, and doing this as the platform for his engagement with them.

---

*Listening God, teach us the ways of gentleness and peace
without losing our focus and passion,
and make us wise for Jesus' sake. Amen.*

ANDY JOHN

An allegory

Tell me, you who desire to be subject to the law, will you not listen to the law? For it is written that Abraham had two sons, one by an enslaved woman and the other by a free woman. One, the child of the enslaved woman, was born according to the flesh; the other, the child of the free woman, was born through the promise. Now this is an allegory: these women are two covenants.

Paul's sojourn into the realms of gentle appeal has been short lived. He returns to the disciplines with which God has blessed him and where he is most comfortable: logic and scripture. In particular, he uses a favoured device to make his point by turning a story from the Old Testament into an allegory.

We should note that Paul expands his point further to emphasise what is troubling him most: salvation is God's free gift, offered on the basis of promise and without any reference to the law. His allegory allows him to place the truth of what he is claiming right back into the Old Testament and supports his contention that Jesus is the fulfilment of what God has always planned since the beginning of time.

However, there is much more to our reading today. We are invited to reflect on how we learn to use the Bible well, become well-versed and confident in our reading. Christians have been known as the 'people of the book'. While we do not worship scripture, apostolic Christianity has always been understood to flow from and connect strongly with the Bible. It is here that we are introduced to Jesus and learn about God's plan for the world. The Bible is the way in which, by God's Spirit, we can deepen our faith and encounter God personally. Paul's grasp of the scriptures and his attention to its commands should invite us to the same rigour and devotion. We should pray that the written word becomes a living word for us each day.

Lord God, help us to become people of the scriptures,
being shaped and blessed in our reading and study,
for Jesus Christ's sake. Amen.

ANDY JOHN

Freedom in Christ

Listen! I, Paul, am telling you that, if you let yourselves be circumcised, Christ will be of no benefit to you. Once again I testify to every man who lets himself be circumcised that he is obliged to obey the entire law. You who want to be reckoned as righteous by the law have cut yourselves off from Christ; you have fallen away from grace. For through the Spirit, by faith, we eagerly wait for the hope of righteousness.

In our reading today, Paul sharpens his argument so that there can be no double standard, no compromise or attempt to 'have it both ways'. In other words, he argues the return to Jewish ritual and custom as a way of sustaining one's life in God cannot sit alongside a commitment to the gospel. Why? Because the obligation of consistency is real. To embrace the demands of the law is to resist the freedom we possess in Christ.

Facing his former friends with an uncompromising choice, Paul raises issues which are not easy to bring to the surface. We do not speak often nor easily about questions of truth and error. Indeed, in our post-modern world the very idea of truth is often pilloried. We are more used to hearing about 'my truth' than any objective standard. Although it is undoubtedly true that perspective is essential and there will be legitimate different points of view, there is great danger in abandoning objective truth as an idea.

Paul was adamant the Galatians were in danger: their version of the faith was distorted, and they had 'cut themselves off from Christ'. So our reading presents us with a challenge too. Faith has content and will shape our understanding and behaviour. If we adopt ideas and practices which move us further from Christ, they will ultimately harm us. The alternative Paul urges is a life based on the promise of God in Jesus and regulated by God's Holy Spirit. How Paul understands this dynamic is something we will consider tomorrow.

Lord God, keep us close to the truth which sets us free and enable us
to make wise and healthy choices as your friends and followers.
For Jesus Christ's sake. Amen.

ANDY JOHN

War of the worlds

Live by the Spirit, I say, and do not gratify the desires of the flesh. For what the flesh desires is opposed to the Spirit, and what the Spirit desires is opposed to the flesh... But if you are led by the Spirit, you are not subject to the law. Now the works of the flesh are obvious... By contrast, the fruit of the Spirit is love, joy, peace, patience, kindness, generosity, faithfulness, gentleness and self-control.

For much of this letter, Paul has argued that the gospel invites a response of faith. We are justified by this response, but only because God has graciously made the invitation. There is no other route available and to try to construct one is doomed to failure. Even the law, good as it is, cannot achieve this, nor was it ever designed to do so.

But his focus now is on another kind of battle. Perhaps Paul senses he could be open to the charge that without a tight framework for living, Christians might end up pleasing their own appetites? Against such a disordered life, he asserts the primacy of a life regulated by God's Holy Spirit. And the contrast is sharp and clear: a life lived on its own terms, without Christ, will be self-absorbed. The 'flesh' will always veer towards what pleases rather than what is needful. However, a life motivated by and sustained through God's Holy Spirit is altogether different. It is marked by those same traits we find in Jesus. In other words, the Holy Spirit of God makes the Christ of God living and real in our experience.

This is not to set scripture against the work of the Spirit. Rather, it is to show that only by God's Spirit can these things truly live and grow in us. What we read and learn therefore in the Bible is animated by God who seeks to fashion the image of Jesus into each of us.

Living God, your Holy Spirit leads us into the life of your Son Jesus Christ.
Make us open to your guiding, strengthen us to respond well
and to follow with courage and devotion. For his sake. Amen.

ANDY JOHN

The cross of Christ

See what large letters I make when I am writing in my own hand! It is those who want to make a good showing in the flesh that try to compel you to be circumcised – only that they may not be persecuted for the cross of Christ. Even the circumcised do not themselves obey the law, but they want you to be circumcised so that they may boast about your flesh. May I never boast of anything except the cross of our Lord Jesus Christ, by which the world has been crucified to me and I to the world.

In our final reading, we see perspectives which help us make sense of Paul's letter. Elsewhere he alludes to a difficulty which seems to be a physical challenge (2 Corinthians 12:7) and may lie behind his exclamation: 'See what large letters I make!' (v. 11). But this inhibition allows Paul to remind the Galatians that those who insist on a physical display of faith do so only to avoid trouble. And their intention in compelling the Galatians is only to take pride that they are now obedient to the law. Paul insists he will take pride in one thing only: the cross.

The physicality of these statements is intriguing. On the one hand Paul lives with his impediment and endures the pain this creates. He has also challenged the Galatians that their reliance on an outward sign of faith undermines their trust in Christ. And yet it is crucifixion which has allowed Paul to live fully for the first time. For Jesus this act of brutality brought the end of his physical life, but Paul has discovered that it has brought him new life.

We have to manage many hardships in our lives. They may be deeply challenging. Paul's final words help us to set them alongside something of supreme importance: the death and resurrection of Jesus. He does not suggest the challenges disappear, but he understands and manages them in the light of this all-important event. My hope and prayer for us all is that we will be able to do the same.

---

*Lord Jesus Christ, you laid down your life for me and by your stripes
I am whole. May I live for you alone. Amen.*

ANDY JOHN

Sowing the seed: parables in Mark

In the past I have heard preachers say 'Christianity is a propositional religion' – that is, that our faith rests on doctrinal statements. This could not be further from the truth: the Bible is a book of stories, and Jesus was a consummate storyteller. Yes, we can draw propositions from these stories, but just as God was 'enfleshed' in Jesus, so our Christian teaching needs to be 'enfleshed' in stories, whether about our own lives or symbolic stories like Jesus' parables.

Stories reach directly into people's hearts and imaginations in a way no theological statement can do. Jesus knew the crowds would listen more readily to stories and go away thinking about their meaning. When the Bible says he taught 'with authority', it does not mean he shouted louder or stated his case more firmly. I think it means he taught with authenticity: his stories rang true, and his life backed them up.

Mark 4:33–34 tells us: 'With many such parables he spoke the word to them as they were able to hear it; he did not speak to them except in parables, but he explained everything in private to his disciples' (NRSV). I wonder why he explained the parables to his disciples? It cannot be because they were more obtuse than the crowds; perhaps it was because they would soon be teaching others, so he needed to make sure they understood the inherent message. I do not think they were meant to go out and explain the parables to the crowds; like Jesus, they too were called to be storytellers, and perhaps even make up their own stories (as we can see Paul and the other epistle writers doing).

Mark, the shortest gospel, has fewer parables than other gospels, and so I have included a few passages not always regarded as parables, but which I think qualify. Like all parables, the ones Mark relates are all about the kingdom of God. He lacks the stories about being lost and found that we find in Luke, but he packs in a lot of parables about sowing seed and the miracle of unexpected growth. These stories are an encouragement to those of us who, to quote Psalm 126:5, 'sow in tears', that we will in time 'reap with joy'.

VERONICA ZUNDEL

The parable of the doctor

Jesus went out again beside the sea; the whole crowd gathered around him, and he taught them. As he was walking along, he saw Levi son of Alphaeus sitting at the tax-collection station, and he said to him, 'Follow me.' And he got up and followed him. And as he sat at dinner in Levi's house, many tax collectors and sinners were also sitting with Jesus and his disciples, for there were many who followed him. When the scribes of the Pharisees saw that he was eating with sinners and tax collectors, they said to his disciples, 'Why does he eat with tax collectors and sinners?' When Jesus heard this, he said to them, 'Those who are well have no need of a physician but those who are sick; I have come to call not the righteous but sinners.'

The UK TV series *Doctor Who*, running for over 60 years, gives us a 'superhero', the Doctor, who wears no cape, carries no gun, seeks peace in all situations and has two hearts – a double dose of compassion? One might almost suspect some Christian inspiration – and indeed, there have been a number of Christian scriptwriters involved over the years.

Jesus comes not to congratulate those who toe the line, but as a doctor to heal the sick in soul, mind and body. Who you shared meals with, in his society, demonstrated your status and reputation. It is not so different now. We have a radio programme in which people fantasise about what famous people today or in the past they would like to eat with. But Jesus chooses to dine with tax collectors (collaborators with the hated Roman occupiers) and sinners (mostly those who were too poor and overworked to observe all the rules about food and cleanliness).

The Pharisees had a mindset in which eating with the 'unrighteous' contaminated a person. So Jesus was surrendering his purity by feasting with these unrespectable people. Yet to Jesus, it was holiness rather than sin that was contagious. By sharing food with the rejected, he was affirming and cleansing them, changing their self-perception from negative to positive.

Am I prepared to mix with people who are not like me –
not to demonstrate how superior I am, but to stand alongside them?

VERONICA ZUNDEL

The parable of the bridegroom

Now John's disciples and the Pharisees were fasting, and people came and said to [Jesus], 'Why do John's disciples and the disciples of the Pharisees fast, but your disciples do not fast?' Jesus said to them, 'The wedding attendants cannot fast while the bridegroom is with them, can they? As long as they have the bridegroom with them, they cannot fast. The days will come when the bridegroom is taken away from them, and then they will fast on that day.'

Fasting has been a part of all religions from time immemorial. I cannot fast because of medication I take, but I know it can help make time for God and concentrate the mind by ignoring the needs of the body.

Jesus however tells his critics that now, while he, 'the bridegroom', is with them, is no time for fasting, but a time for feasting. No one fasts at a wedding! John the Baptist's disciples fast because his ministry is focused on turning one's life around and beginning to obey the call of God. Jesus' ministry is about rejoicing at the grace of God, celebrating the one in whom people meet God in a unique way. The theologian and songwriter John Bell of the Iona Community gives a talk entitled 'Jesus was a fat man' in which he dismantles the idea of a thin ascetic Jesus and portrays him as a man who was always feasting.

What does it mean to us to see Jesus as a bridegroom? It is a very intimate, personal image, coming to its culmination in Revelation 21:2: 'And I saw the holy city, the new Jerusalem, coming down out of heaven from God, prepared as a bride adorned for her husband.' The church is the bride of Christ, which does not make it a subordinate servant, but a much-loved partner in life. As our bridegroom, Jesus is the one who has chosen us specially to live and work with him in the transforming of the world.

Jesus, show me when it is time to feast and time to fast. Amen.

VERONICA ZUNDEL

Parables of stretching

'No one sews a piece of unshrunk cloth on an old cloak; otherwise, the patch pulls away from it, the new from the old, and a worse tear is made. Similarly, no one puts new wine into old wineskins; otherwise, the wine will burst the skins, and the wine is lost, and so are the skins, but one puts new wine into fresh wineskins.'

A leak of acid in our boiler cupboard, which doubled as an airing cupboard, made huge holes in some of my favourite, and newest, nightdresses (we have a new boiler now). I tried sewing them up but wearing them just stretched the mended area till it unpicked again. Meanwhile, bottles of prosecco or sparkling soft drinks, laid in the 'wine rack' in my fridge, have repeatedly bubbled up and popped out their corks, flooding the fridge with sticky liquid. I have had to find space for them to stand upright in the fridge door.

It is not easy to accommodate the new. People are attached to their old routines and customs; they feel secure with them. But Jesus declares that his kingdom is all new and needs new forms to hold it. It cannot just be patched on to the old way of doing things (the Jewish law) or crammed into old containers. It is too stretchable, too 'fizzy', for that. 'You have heard that it was said to those of ancient times… But I say to you…' (Matthew 5:21–22ff).

Churches have been saying for some time that for a changing society, the church and its habits need to change. Too often, it seems to me, we have been trying to put old wine into new wineskins: changing the outside but not the inside. We need to change, not just our tune, but the kind of words we put to it. 'Jesus Christ is the same yesterday and today and forever' (Hebrews 13:8) doesn't mean the church has to be!

Perhaps the first stage in this process is *listening*. What questions is the world asking? What experiences and dimensions of life is it missing?

What if church radically changed its way of meeting,
the contents of its meetings, even its place of meeting?
Might that make it a less alien, intimidating space?

VERONICA ZUNDEL

The parable of the strong man

Then [Jesus] went home, and the crowd came together again, so that they could not even eat. When his family heard it, they went out to restrain him, for people were saying, 'He has gone out of his mind.' And the scribes who came down from Jerusalem said, 'He has Beelzebul, and by the ruler of the demons he casts out demons.' And he called them to him and spoke to them in parables, 'How can Satan cast out Satan? If a kingdom is divided against itself, that kingdom cannot stand... And if Satan has risen up against himself and is divided, he cannot stand, but his end has come. But no one can enter a strong man's house and plunder his property without first tying up the strong man; then indeed the house can be plundered.'

Ched Myers' political exploration of Mark's gospel is called *Binding the Strong Man* (a shorter, simpler version is *Say to this Mountain*, Orbis Books, 1996). It is easy to see how this particular parable can be read politically, so that it is not just about 'demon possession'. The idolisation of the 'strong man' (and it usually is a man) as a political leader is alive and well today. But Jesus points out that it is unwise to use the strategies of the 'strong leader' to unseat him: two 'strong men' fighting each other will usually destroy each other.

How, then, do we combat the forces of evil, whether political or personal, in our society? What does Jesus mean by 'tying up' the strong man? I think in the context of the rest of his teaching and ministry, he means that evil can only be cast out by love and prayer (see Mark 9:28–29). Love and prayer undermine the work of the 'evil one' because they are a surprise to him, unfamiliar to his way of thinking.

Some images of Jesus portray him as a kind of wrestling hero, a muscular superman who can literally 'beat the hell' out of his opponents. This could not be further from the Jesus of the gospels, who overcomes through apparent weakness, tying up his critics in knots with his creative stories and tactics.

Prince of Peace, teach me the ways of peace,
that overcome strongholds. Amen.

VERONICA ZUNDEL

The parable of the seed

[Jesus] began to teach them many things in parables, and in his teaching he said to them: 'Listen! A sower went out to sow. And as he sowed, some seed fell on a path, and the birds came and ate it up. Other seed fell on rocky ground, where it did not have much soil, and it sprang up quickly, since it had no depth of soil. And when the sun rose, it was scorched, and since it had no root it withered away. Other seed fell among thorns, and the thorns grew up and choked it, and it yielded no grain. Other seed fell into good soil and brought forth grain, growing up and increasing and yielding thirty and sixty and a hundredfold.' And he said, 'If you have ears to hear, then hear!'

As a woodworker, Jesus had probably made ploughs for farmers to prepare the ground before sowing their seed. He was not a farmer himself, but he lived in an agrarian society and he knew that, as a panellist on BBC Radio 4's *Gardener's Question Time* used to say many years ago: 'The answer lies in the soil.'

We know from frequent distressing reports in the news that if a harvest fails, famine is only a step away. The Bible is also full of accounts of drought and famine, from the story of Joseph in Egypt to Naomi and her husband who flee famine in the book of Ruth. Even in the well-fed west, where we behave as though food comes directly from supermarkets, recent shortages have brought home to us that disruption in the processes of growth or supply chains can endanger our varied diet.

Jesus' immediate disciples were fishermen, although many of those who followed him were farmers or smallholders. Perhaps Peter, Andrew, James and John had not thought much about the agricultural food chain: they relied on there always being fish in the sea, though even this supply could fail at times. The reality is, sowing physical or spiritual seed is always a risk: yields of 'thirty and sixty and a hundredfold' such as Jesus predicts (v. 8) were beyond people's wildest imaginings. No wonder they did not quite understand this parable.

What 'seed' have you sown in your life,
from which you are waiting for a harvest?

VERONICA ZUNDEL

Listen very carefully

And [Jesus] said to them, 'Do you not understand this parable? Then how will you understand all the parables? The sower sows the word. These are the ones on the path where the word is sown: when they hear, Satan immediately comes and takes away the word that is sown in them. And these are the ones sown on rocky ground: when they hear the word, they immediately receive it with joy. But they have no root and endure only for a while; then, when trouble or persecution arises on account of the word, immediately they fall away. And others are those sown among the thorns: these are the ones who hear the word, but the cares of the age and the lure of wealth and the desire for other things come in and choke the word, and it yields nothing. And these are the ones sown on the good soil: they hear the word and accept it and bear fruit, thirty and sixty and a hundredfold.'

'I've told you that already', my husband often says to me. And I say the same to him. The fact is, we hear selectively and whether we truly listen depends not only on the importance of what we are hearing, but also on what else is going on around at the time.

But where are we in this parable? Some preachers suggest we are the seed, good or bad; some say we are the soil. Jesus' interpretation, or Matthew's memory, are not entirely clear. I favour the understanding that we are the soil, but I do not think it really matters: the key point is that the word of God is sown into different circumstances, and people in those different circumstances receive it differently. Some are, we might say, 'hard of hearing', and the seed sown on our hard ears and hearts is immediately snatched away. Some are shallow, unprepared for the Christian life to bring sorrow as well as joy, so their faith fails to endure in hardship. Some have lives already cluttered with possessions, plans and dreams and find it hard to focus on God's call. And some are 'good soil' – ploughed over, watered, ready to bear a harvest.

As God's 'holy ones', what does it take to be fertile soil
for God's message? How do we prepare?

VERONICA ZUNDEL

The parable of the lamp

[Jesus] said to them, 'Is a lamp brought in to be put under the bushel basket or under the bed and not on the lampstand? For there is nothing hidden, except to be disclosed; nor is anything secret, except to come to light. If you have ears to hear, then hear!' And he said to them, 'Pay attention to what you hear; the measure you give will be the measure you get, and it will be added to you. For to those who have, more will be given, and from those who have nothing, even what they have will be taken away.'

'Do not hide your light under a bushel' is a saying that has passed from the Bible into our everyday speech. Television talent contests encourage people to demonstrate their skills in singing, dancing or even comedy, and sometimes they uncover people of exceptional talent who go on to dazzling careers. Nevertheless, you do not have to have performing skills to 'shine your light' and make a difference to others' lives. The important thing is to use whatever gifts you have, whether it is cooking, caring for others or leading prayers. A lamp is made for shining, not for hiding.

As a writer I find this difficult. For me the joy is in the writing, not in the process of getting it published and sold. I want to share it, but I find the challenge of getting it 'out there' quite hard. Are you a 'shrinking violet' when it comes to putting yourself forward for tasks? This is where encouraging friends can be a great help, saying, 'I think you could do that well.' Remember also that exposing your abilities to the world is a kind of humility – we risk failing, but we have to take that risk to use what we have been given.

Perhaps that is also the point of Jesus' rather frightening warning that what we give will be what we get (and more); while if we give nothing, we gain nothing. Gifts are not to be hoarded but to be shared; bread kept in the basket will just go stale or mouldy.

Lord Jesus, give me the courage to risk failing,
rather than never trying to shine. Amen.

VERONICA ZUNDEL

The parable of the sleeping sower

[Jesus] also said, 'The kingdom of God is as if someone would scatter seed on the ground and would sleep and rise night and day, and the seed would sprout and grow, he does not know how. The earth produces of itself first the stalk, then the head, then the full grain in the head. But when the grain is ripe, at once he goes in with his sickle because the harvest has come.'

A good gardener will not plant seeds and then dig the newly sprouting plants up every few days to see how they are doing. That is a guaranteed way to kill them! Essentially, Jesus is saying that building the kingdom of God, like sowing seed, is an act of faith. We cast out a line (to change the metaphor!) and then wait patiently till something bites. We speak some words we think must be spoken or we pray a daring prayer for our friend or neighbour or church, and then we wait for it to come to fruition. And it may take years.

The trouble is, we are getting too used to instant results. It is hard to wait even a few minutes for a file to download. Ironically, this is happening when we live longer than ever, and actually have far more time to wait for things! But we try to cram more and more into our lives and lose the ability to wait for anything.

Jesus' parable suggests that the most fruitful times in our lives may be the times when we think we are doing nothing. If we have sown a seed, whether professionally, in witnessing to a friend or in trying to resolve a difficult situation, worry will not actually help it grow. We can sleep and rise, all the time knowing that God will be working to bring about what is best for the kingdom (which may not be what *we* think is best).

This was why Jesus himself was able to withdraw, with or without his closest disciples, to quiet places to rest and recover from his ministry. He had confidence that the outcome was safe in his Father's hands.

What 'green shoots' of God's kingdom can you see growing
in your church, workplace, area or world?

VERONICA ZUNDEL

The Fourth Sunday before Advent

The mustard seed

[Jesus] also said, 'With what can we compare the kingdom of God, or what parable will we use for it? It is like a mustard seed, which, when sown upon the ground, is the smallest of all the seeds on earth, yet when it is sown it grows up and becomes the greatest of all shrubs and puts forth large branches, so that the birds of the air can make nests in its shade.' With many such parables he spoke the word to them as they were able to hear it; he did not speak to them except in parables, but he explained everything in private to his disciples.

I like small churches. I like the fact that in a small church you can know everyone's name and at least a little about them. In a big church you can be a bit anonymous (but of course some people like that, at least when they are 'dipping their toes in the water'). However, unless a small church learns how to grow, in numbers as well as depth of discipleship, it will always live on the edge of closing down, as my beloved Mennonite church did.

Jesus' closest disciples might have been discouraged at the fact that while large crowds followed him, few committed themselves to him in the way they had. Or the wider crowd might have been asking 'Where is this kingdom of God then? We cannot see many signs of it yet.' He answers with this well-known parable about the tiny seed that grows into a large shrub, almost a tree, where birds can make their home. What is perhaps less well known is that mustard, of the kind he is talking about, is essentially a garden pest. It grows everywhere you do not want it to, rather like the self-sown ash trees that have colonised my garden. Essentially, the kingdom of God is subversive. It insinuates its invasive roots into the garden of 'how we've always done things' and creates cracks in the world system that benefits some and oppresses others.

The mustard seed parable not only creates hope for growth but also calls us to be innovative, radical and overturn the carefully laid plans of the world.

How could we as disciples be more mustard-seed-like?

VERONICA ZUNDEL

The parable of outside and inside

Then [Jesus] called the crowd again and said to them, 'Listen to me, all of you, and understand: there is nothing outside a person that by going in can defile, but the things that come out are what defile.' When he had left the crowd and entered the house, his disciples asked him about the parable. He said to them, 'So, are you also without understanding? Do you not see that whatever goes into a person from outside cannot defile, since it enters not the heart but the stomach and goes out into the sewer?' (Thus he declared all foods clean.) And he said, 'It is what comes out of a person that defiles. For it is from within, from the human heart, that evil intentions come: sexual immorality, theft, murder, adultery, avarice, wickedness, deceit, debauchery, envy, slander, pride, folly. All these evil things come from within, and they defile a person.'

A little Jewish girl I know came home from a schoolfriend's party and declared, 'Mummy, I ate a Christian sausage.' (Her mum was not too disturbed.) 'How can young people keep their way pure?' asks Psalm 119:9. The traditional answer has been by avoiding things that might corrupt you. For the Jews of Jesus' day (and some Jews today), alongside many rules about cleanliness, there were strict food rules, and the 'wrong' food could defile a person and lead to a need for special cleansing.

Jesus had no time for 'purity culture'. The trouble is, the search for purity usually leads to excluding not just foods but also people one regards as contaminating. Yet Jesus touched those with leprosy, as well as dead bodies, such as Jairus' daughter (Mark 5:41). He believed his power to cleanse was greater than their power to contaminate.

Where then do our 'evil intentions' come from? The sermon on the mount (Matthew 5—7) suggests that they come from our attitudes: 'You have heard that it was said to those of ancient times, "You shall not murder," and "whoever murders shall be liable to judgement." But I say to you that if you are angry with a brother or sister, you will be liable to judgement' (Matthew 5:21–22a). Repentance is not just a change of behaviour, but a change of attitude too.

Holy Spirit, give me contagious holiness. Amen.

VERONICA ZUNDEL

The parable of the yeast

Now the disciples had forgotten to bring any bread; and they had only one loaf with them in the boat. And [Jesus] cautioned them, saying, 'Watch out – beware of the yeast of the Pharisees and the yeast of Herod.' They said to one another, 'It is because we have no bread.' And becoming aware of it, Jesus said to them, 'Why are you talking about having no bread? Do you still not perceive or understand? Are your hearts hardened? Do you have eyes and fail to see? Do you have ears and fail to hear? And do you not remember? When I broke the five loaves for the five thousand, how many baskets full of broken pieces did you collect?' They said to him, 'Twelve.' 'And the seven for the four thousand, how many baskets full of broken pieces did you collect?' And they said to him, 'Seven.' Then he said to them, 'Do you not yet understand?'

One can barely blame the disciples for not understanding this parable – it is not easy! I think it is something like this: yeast in the New Testament is an ambivalent symbol. In other gospels, Jesus uses it as a parable of the 'infiltrating' nature of God's kingdom – 'The kingdom of heaven is like yeast that a woman took and mixed in with three measures of flour until all of it was leavened' (Matthew 13:33). Meanwhile, we know that in the context of Passover, yeast is something that must be radically eliminated, hence leading the Jews to invent spring cleaning!

Perhaps what Jesus means by 'the yeast of the Pharisees' is their exploiting religion to gain power over others: 'They tie up heavy burdens, hard to bear, and lay them on the shoulders of others, but they themselves are unwilling to lift a finger to move them' (Matthew 23:4). One can easily find modern parallels. And the 'yeast of Herod' is perhaps his misuse of political power. These are both temptations common to those we put into leadership, especially the leaders of large organisations.

Jesus contrasts these 'yeasts' with the abundant provision of God to those who have nothing. We do not have to provide for ourselves: God provides.

God's kingdom is one of abundance, not of scarcity.

VERONICA ZUNDEL

The parable of the stumbling block

'If any of you cause one of these little ones who believe in me to sin, it would be better for you if a great millstone were hung around your neck and you were thrown into the sea. If your hand causes you to sin, cut it off; it is better for you to enter life maimed than to have two hands and to go to hell, to the unquenchable fire. And if your foot causes you to sin, cut it off; it is better for you to enter life lame than to have two feet and to be thrown into hell. And if your eye causes you to stumble, tear it out; it is better for you to enter the kingdom of God with one eye than to have two eyes and to be thrown into hell, where their worm never dies and the fire is never quenched.'

When Jesus talks of 'little ones' he usually means not children, but the poor and the outcasts who are the majority of those who follow him. But we know that he placed children at the centre of his ministry too, and urged us to imitate them. So perhaps 'little ones' encompasses all the vulnerable who trust Jesus to lead them and keep them safe.

Sadly, I have read much news lately of those who have lost their faith or had to reconstruct it with much pain, because of the bad behaviour of Christian leaders or the judgementalism of other Christians. Abuse, whether it is physical, sexual or spiritual, is a great destroyer of faith and trust. It is a 'stumbling block' to anyone who encounters Jesus through people who later turn out to be untrustworthy. Leaders especially, but all God's people, must act with integrity.

In the early centuries of the church, some male spiritual leaders literally castrated themselves to avoid sexual sin. I really do not think that is what Jesus intends here! We may however have to remove ourselves from influences that lead us into wrongdoing, or make drastic decisions in our lives to enable change. The central point is, it is better to endure losses now, than to lose our spiritual life by harming others.

How can I, and my church, best protect the 'little ones'?

VERONICA ZUNDEL

The parable of the vineyard

Then [Jesus] began to speak to them in parables. 'A man planted a vineyard, put a fence around it, dug a pit for the wine press, and built a watchtower; then he leased it to tenants and went away. When the season came, he sent a slave to the tenants to collect from them his share of the produce of the vineyard. But they seized him and beat him and sent him away empty-handed... And so it was with many others; some they beat, and others they killed. He had still one other, a beloved son. Finally he sent him to them, saying, "They will respect my son." But those tenants said to one another, "This is the heir; come, let us kill him, and the inheritance will be ours." So they seized him, killed him, and threw him out of the vineyard. What then will the owner of the vineyard do? He will come and destroy the tenants and give the vineyard to others.'

The vineyard is a common symbol throughout the Bible for the 'chosen people' of Israel. Here Jesus gives a potent summary of how they have failed in their mission to be 'a light to the nations'. He casts himself as the ultimate prophet, not just a servant of God but God's own Son, whom the people will both beat and kill.

We need to be careful how we interpret this parable, especially its ending. On one side, we should not conclude that the Christian church has superseded the Jewish nation and that God has no further purpose for them. Romans 9—11 makes it clear that the Jews still have a role in God's plans. As a Jew by birth myself, the longer I follow Jesus, the more I value my Jewish heritage.

On the other hand, we should not believe that the current state of Israel maps exactly to the ancient chosen people. Throughout biblical history, possession of the land was always conditional on acting justly, and we should call all nations to that.

I think Jesus is issuing a warning here, that simply being God's chosen is not a free pass to ignore God's commands. We need to demonstrate our chosenness by our behaviour.

What does it mean to you to be chosen?

VERONICA ZUNDEL

An acted parable

While they were eating, [Jesus] took a loaf of bread, and after blessing it he broke it, gave it to them, and said, 'Take; this is my body.' Then he took a cup, and after giving thanks he gave it to them, and all of them drank from it. He said to them, 'This is my blood of the covenant, which is poured out for many. Truly I tell you, I will never again drink of the fruit of the vine until that day when I drink it new in the kingdom of God.'

Whatever you call it – the Eucharist, Communion, the Lord's Supper – you may not think of this act of breaking and sharing as a parable. Yet it is, in a sense, a story that Jesus is acting out about the meaning of his death. If, as three of the gospels make explicit and the fourth suggests, this is a Passover meal, he is also linking his coming suffering to the great defining story of the Jewish people, their liberation from slavery in Egypt. He is saying, as his forerunner John the Baptist does, 'Here is the Lamb of God' (John 1:29) – that his death is a sacrifice that will free his people.

Jesus is also inaugurating a new covenant – and the Old Testament demonstrates amply that in the Jewish tradition every covenant is sealed with a blood sacrifice. This may seem archaic and strange to us, yet for centuries children, and indeed adults, would declare their friendship by mingling their blood and proclaiming themselves 'blood brothers/sisters'. There is something deep in the human psyche that responds to this symbolism.

Just as we need to tell stories in our worship and witness, to reach the hearts of our listeners, so perhaps we also need to perform symbolic actions to convey our faith. Some will do this through 'bells and smells', traditions that express 'the beauty of holiness'; others through puppets, dance or even scientific demonstrations. I once started a sermon by thinly slicing a white cabbage. I can assure you it was relevant!

There are three ways Jesus is like a Jewish mother:
he uses food to express love; he tells us not to worry,
he'll do the worrying for us; and he never lets go!

VERONICA ZUNDEL

Habakkuk

We might ask what a short book of 56 verses, probably written 600 years before Christ's birth, has to do with us. We know nothing about its author (except his name) and there is little detail about his location, his people or the enemies he faces. Habakkuk has no great revelation to offer about God's involvement with the world; indeed, he seems to repeatedly question if God will intervene at all. Violence and injustice seem to rage around, there are hints of famine and hunger stalking the land, and there is little respect for legal authority.

Of course, these are not issues that are unique to Habakkuk's time and place. We have had, in recent times, to come to terms with a pandemic and its continuing effects upon individuals and institutions, an economic downturn and ongoing armed conflicts. Some very public failings have made many distrustful of politicians and political systems, while there seems to be a lingering sense of widespread anxiety. What might we have to deal with next?

The fascinating thing about this book is that it does not attempt to give answers. There are no instructions to Habakkuk's people that will enable them to lead a more godly life and ensure their salvation. There are no prophetic promises of divine intervention, the destruction of enemies and the ensuring of a lasting peace. In fact, nothing much happens. Habakkuk poses the sort of questions that we all at times might ask of God: are you there? Why don't you do something? Do you care? Yet God does not always answer. The whole text is an exercise in internal reflection that might hope for external replies, but which does not expect them.

Yet despite all this, Habakkuk keeps on asking questions. He refuses not only to pretend that everything is, after all, alright, but also to submit to despair. There is a righteous anger that Habakkuk directs towards God as well as his enemies, but there is also a deeply rooted faith that insists that God's vision for the 'appointed time' will come to fruition and will not be unnecessarily delayed. In the end, Habakkuk insists, we will see God's glory cover the whole earth 'as the waters cover the sea' (2:14). That will be worth waiting for.

AMANDA BLOOR

Look and see

O Lord, how long shall I cry for help, and you will not listen? Or cry to you, 'Violence!' and you will not save? Why do you make me see wrongdoing and look at trouble? Destruction and violence are before me; strife and contention arise. So the law becomes slack, and justice never prevails. The wicked surround the righteous; therefore judgement comes forth perverted. Look at the nations and see! Be astonished! Be astounded!

'God sees everything,' we assure ourselves. We are told in the scriptures that we are loved, that we are valuable, that we all matter. We pray for support, and we hold before God those people and places which suffer. Yet there are times when things go badly wrong, when we or others need help, and when injustice seems to rage around. We can be tempted, like Habakkuk, to cry out, 'How long, Lord?'

It is easy to empathise with the prophet's pain. Habakkuk seems to wonder if God is really interested in the well-being of humanity and if God chooses not to listen to the cries of creation. It is exhausting to be caught in the middle of violence and destruction that appears to be out of control, and it is distressing to see the suffering of individuals and communities. How much can one person bear?

Yet there is a bigger question there, and it is one that we are required to ask of ourselves when in similar circumstances. 'Why, Lord, do you make me look at this?' asks Habakkuk. The answer might well come back, 'In order to do something about it!' As St Teresa of Ávila pointed out, *we* are Christ's hands here on earth and so it is crucial that trust in God's saving presence does not turn to passivity and disengagement. It is not sufficient just to look at a situation – we are not simply observers – it is crucial also to *see* and then to respond. If God (as we believe) cares, then so must we.

God our hope, in difficult circumstances help us to look and to really see,
to recognise what is necessary and to know what to do. Guide us
and give us strength, so that your justice may prevail. Amen.

AMANDA BLOOR

There is a plan!

I will stand at my watchpost and station myself on the rampart; I will keep watch to see what he will say to me and what he will answer concerning my complaint. Then the Lord answered me and said: Write the vision; make it plain on tablets, so that a runner may read it. For there is still a vision for the appointed time; it speaks of the end and does not lie. If it seems to tarry, wait for it; it will surely come, it will not delay.

Have you ever attended a school performance in which a young child you know is taking part? If so, you will probably have spotted them looking out across the audience, keen to spot that you are there. They might look anxious, unsure if anyone will come to support them, or they might be confidently searching for the person they know will not let them down. Either way, when they recognise your face, they are likely to beam with delight that you are there and all is well.

Our relationship with God can follow similar lines, often influenced by the experiences we have had, especially if they affect our ability to trust. In this passage, the prophet seems to be trying to convince himself that God will be present; that God's promise is reliable and true. Like a soldier patrolling the ramparts of the city, the prophet looks out and waits until he can see ahead. Will his faith be rewarded, will help be on its way? Then the Lord speaks: 'I have a plan and it will happen. Be patient and wait for the right time.'

It is never easy to wait, especially when we look around us and clearly see the need for God's presence. Perhaps we, like Habakkuk, need to learn patience, drawing comfort from faith that God has a vision and it will be achieved.

Lord, sometimes I strain my eyes looking into the darkness for signs of your light. It is hard to hold on, to know that you are there and that you do have a plan. Help me to be patient and to trust in your love. Amen.

AMANDA BLOOR

Actions and consequences

'Alas for you who heap up what is not your own!' How long will you load yourselves with goods taken in pledge? Will not your own creditors suddenly rise and those who make you tremble wake up? Then you will be plunder for them. Because you have plundered many nations, all who survive of the peoples shall plunder you – because of human bloodshed and violence to the earth, to cities and all who live in them.

We live in a society whereby we expect to have the things we want whenever we want them. An economic downturn might make us think more about our finances before clicking the 'buy' button on a website or taking something to the checkout, but if we can afford it, it can be difficult to resist an impulse purchase. We expect to have sufficient electricity to light our homes and power our devices, limitless clean water to drink, heating to keep us warm and a choice of foods – in and out of season – to eat. This, for many of us, is normality. It is only when something disrupts the provision of goods or services that we give them thought.

Yet Habakkuk's words about plundering many nations bring me face-to-face with the reality that my behaviour has consequences for others. Ridiculously low prices for clothing means that people elsewhere pay the price: the machinists who are badly remunerated for skilled work, the villages where water sources are contaminated by chemical runoff and the land put out of use when cheap clothes are simply dumped after one wearing. Using the planet's resources carelessly not only means high bills for individuals, but also damages God's creation. Climate change disproportionally affects people living in poorer parts of the world, leading to flooding, air pollution, loss of land because of rising sea levels and the increased spread of some infectious diseases. Greed and thoughtless consumption on one side of the world can indeed do violence to the earth and its peoples. May God give us grace to recognise this and change our ways.

Generous God, you give us so much and it's easy to become complacent with our prosperity. Help us to realise that our actions affect others so that we may act with care and conscience. Amen.

AMANDA BLOOR

The glory of the Lord shines out

The very stones will cry out from the wall, and the rafter will respond from the woodwork. 'Alas for you who build a town by bloodshed and found a city on iniquity!' Is it not from the Lord of hosts that peoples labour only to feed the flames and nations weary themselves for nothing? But the earth will be filled with the knowledge of the glory of the Lord, as the waters cover the sea.

I find it remarkable that Habakkuk is so conscious of God's presence throughout the created world that even inanimate objects (in this case, the stones that form a wall and the beams of the rafters) cry out against greed and iniquity. There is nowhere that is not touched by God's desire for justice and righteousness; nothing that can hide human iniquity from God's view.

We hear again in this passage the passionate desire of the prophet that his people will change their ways for the better. Towns built on 'bloodshed' and cities founded on 'iniquity' are a tragic indictment of a lack of concern for others and the absence of a moral compass that would challenge such unjust behaviour. God, the prophet reminds his people, knows that they are expending energy to no good purpose. Their actions will have no positive outcome.

It would be easy at this point to simply give up, as greed, carelessness and violence seem to have the upper hand. Yet that is not the prophetic way. It is not God's way either. If the very stones from the walls are crying out, then the call to change is still being heard and there is the possibility that there will be repentance and amendment of life. Habakkuk believes that God is present, and he trusts that God will be recognised. The knowledge of God's glory will fill the whole earth, spreading across the land as water spreads to form the sea. Justice will prevail.

Lord Jesus Christ, God with us, you experienced the toxic effects of iniquity and bloodshed. Open our eyes so that we may see God's glory in all places. Make us agents of change and advocates of peace. Amen.

AMANDA BLOOR

Worthless idols

What use is an idol once its maker has shaped it – a cast image, a teacher of lies? For its maker trusts in what has been made, though the product is only an idol that cannot speak! Alas for you who say to the wood, 'Wake up!' to silent stone, 'Rouse yourself!' Can it teach? See, it is gold and silver plated, and there is no breath in it at all. But the Lord is in his holy temple; let all the earth keep silence before him!

We probably believe that we are too sophisticated to worship figures made of wood and plated with gold and silver. But I wonder if we recognise that there are other things that we can be tempted to turn into idols? I remember being in my early teens and being fascinated by pop stars and Hollywood actors, people who seemed glamorous, successful and popular. Magazines shared carefully selected details about their lives: their favourite foods, their family members and friends, their hobbies and even the colours they preferred to wear. I drank it all in, hoping to become a little like that person and a little less like myself. It is no exaggeration to say that I idolised them. As an adult, I recognise that different aspirations are offered to me, promoted largely by those who have something to sell: a different lifestyle, a better car, a bigger house. It is easy to become dissatisfied and overlook the many blessings I already have.

This passage encourages us to consider the things in which we place our trust and to look beneath the surface glitter. Idols, whatever form they take, cannot give us the things we really need; only God can do that. The passage challenges us too. Do we have form and substance, or are we, like idols, all outward appearance? Do we have the depth that comes from a mature spiritual relationship with the Lord, before whom the noisy chatter of the whole earth is silenced?

Loving God, you give us the things we need and guide us into ways of truth and peace. Grant us the discernment to turn away from idols, so that we may draw closer to you. Amen.

AMANDA BLOOR

God of power and might

In fury you marched on the earth, in anger you trampled nations. You came forth to save your people, to save your anointed. You crushed the head of the wicked house, laying it bare from foundation to roof… I hear, and I tremble within; my lips quiver at the sound. Rottenness enters my bones, and my steps tremble beneath me. I wait quietly for the day of calamity to come upon the people who attack us.

Do we, I wonder, hold conflicted views about God's nature? The Bible tells us repeatedly about a God of love and forgiveness, but sometimes we are faced with passages such as the one above, which describes divine wrath and the consequent destruction of peoples and places. This can lead us to an unhealthy imbalance in our understanding. We know that God is much more than we can conceive, but it is easy to imagine God in terms of human people we know. And some significant figures in our own lives, or examples of earthly leaders, might be profoundly unhelpful models of what power and influence look like.

What is important to remember here, I believe, is that Habakkuk is recognising that God is deeply involved with humanity and that violence and injustice will not be allowed to prevail. The prophet's cry is not one of fear and trembling at God's presence, but an affirmation that God is present and that wickedness, in the end, will not triumph. Which of us, after all, like Habakkuk has not prayed in moments of distress that our persecutors will be punished for the distress that they have inflicted upon us? Yet even in this maelstrom of fear and emotion, Habakkuk holds on to the knowledge that he is loved by God, that he will be saved and that this terrible time will come to an end.

God of power and might, be with us, we pray, when we are beset
by danger and fear. Remind us that we are valuable to you and grant that
we and all your children may live in freedom and quietness.
We ask this through Jesus Christ, Prince of Peace. Amen.

AMANDA BLOOR

Holding on

Though the fig tree does not blossom, and no fruit is on the vines; though the produce of the olive fails and the fields yield no food; though the flock is cut off from the fold and there is no herd in the stalls, yet will I rejoice in the Lord; I will exult in the God of my salvation. God, the Lord, is my strength; he makes my feet like the feet of a deer and makes me tread upon the heights.

We all love a happy ending, with everything tied up neatly and brought to a proper conclusion. Sadly, life is not always like that. The short book of Habakkuk comes to an end without completing the story; the prophet still prays that God will defend his people against those who are intent upon violence, he still trembles for fear of the future and he still has a heart set on retribution.

Food is short because the land is showing the after-effects of sustained aggression. Domesticated animals are cut off from places of shelter and fodder, and harvests are failing, perhaps because there is no one to nurture vines and plant crops. Enemies are close at hand and peace is a distant hope.

It would be understandable if Habakkuk lost heart, blamed God and turned away from religion. We often see that in our own times when tragedies or calamities happen and people ask, 'Where was God?' It is easy to empathise with those who have suffered greatly and have, as a result, lost their faith, and we might ourselves have gone through periods when God seems far off. Yet remarkably, Habakkuk is able to trust God and rejoices in the Lord, whom he describes as his strength and his salvation. Despite all that has happened and the uncertain future, the prophet sings of hope and transformation. I wonder if we, in an uncertain world, can do the same?

Great and generous God, give us strength and courage to face difficulty and disaster. Help us to hold on to faith in your love for us and your continuing presence, even when everything seems to be against us. Give us resurrection hope, through Christ who brings us into new life. Amen.

AMANDA BLOOR

Matthew 8—9

It is not often we can turn to a set of readings which carry us more or less uninterrupted through scripture. So this fortnight we shall confine ourselves to just Matthew 8 and 9, from which there is much to unpack. These two chapters are action-packed with one incident after another, a miracle-filled travelogue as Jesus goes from one place to another, on what comes across as a relentless rush of ministry. People approach him, interrupt him, press in on him. As well as giving us a sense of how busy he was, these mini-episodes (known as pericopes in the biblical studies trade) also give us insight into how first-century Palestinians lived, struggled, suffered and died. In this they are so like us, and yet, the world of first-century Palestine seems so long ago, so far away.

In this set of scenes in the two acts that are chapters 8 and 9, we have a very mixed, multitudinous cast of friends, family, strangers and pilgrims. If we forget for a moment what Jesus did for them, we notice who they are, their needs, desires and fears. In this they are not unlike us, in a society where the damaged and outcasts are ignored, dismissed or just overlooked as being too complicated to deal with. Jesus does deal with them, pastorally, and we see how it takes its toll, just as it does for all those brave and caring people today who minister in mind, body or spirit to those in physical, mental or spiritual distress.

If you read a commentary on Matthew's gospel, it will likely say that the miracles which make up chapters 8 and 9 are an anthology of related kinds of miracles: three healings; three miracles of power; three miracles of restoration. The purpose is to reveal Jesus' power of healing, his authority over nature and his authority over unclean spirits. In this century we might think of medicine, natural disaster and mental health: three aspects of life that still have the capacity to cause great concern.

It is that concern which I want to focus on this fortnight – the care that Christ our good shepherd shows – the pastoral care for the flock which characterises this rollercoaster ride through the downsides of both first-century and modern life.

GORDON GILES

Healing touch

When Jesus came down from the mountainside, large crowds followed him. A man with leprosy came and knelt before him and said, 'Lord, if you are willing, you can make me clean.' Jesus reached out his hand and touched the man. 'I am willing,' he said. 'Be clean!' Immediately he was cleansed of his leprosy. Then Jesus said to him, 'See that you don't tell anyone. But go, show yourself to the priest and offer the gift Moses commanded, as a testimony to them.'

The mountain that Jesus comes down is the mount of the sermon: Jesus has been teaching with authority for three chapters (Matthew 5—7), and now, having heard of his words, we hear of the authority of his actions. Great crowds have heard him preach, and now they follow him, in curiosity perhaps, to see whether he practises what he preaches. They have heard what he *says*, now they want to see what he can *do*.

This is where the choice comes in; the first in line is the leper. Officially an outcast, we wonder at the fact that he is in the midst of the crowds, stepping forward. He tests Jesus, because he is a health hazard physically and spiritually. One wonders how the crowds felt when they saw him. They would have instinctively recoiled. Perhaps they distanced themselves. They probably also held their breath. What would this preacher do? Would he send him away, reject him and quote scripture at him?

Jesus acts with integrity and pastoral love. He sees the problem as an opportunity: 'I am willing', he says (v. 3), and he combines caution and compassion by touching the leper with an outstretched hand. To touch is to risk defilement and disease, but at arm's length the risk is reduced (but not removed). It is a brave and bold and sets a new model for pastoral care.

During Covid, medics, clergy and even family could not touch loved ones in those hours when they needed it most. Touch is healing in its own right, and while there are often good physical and emotional reasons to inhibit people from touching one another, this pericope reminds us that sometimes words and deeds need to go hand in hand, albeit at arm's length.

Lord Jesus, touch us with your love that we may bring your healing to a frightened world. Amen.

GORDON GILES

Remote control

The centurion answered, 'Lord, I am not worthy to have you come under my roof, but only speak the word, and my servant will be healed. For I also am a man under authority, with soldiers under me, and I say to one, "Go," and he goes, and to another, "Come," and he comes, and to my slave, "Do this," and the slave does it.' When Jesus heard him, he was amazed and said to those who followed him, 'Truly I tell you, in no one in Israel have I found such faith.'

In Capernaum Jesus meets a man who is excluded not by infectious disease like the leper, but by his ethnicity. He is Lebanese or Syrian, a Gentile member of Herod's army, policing Palestine under the ultimate authority of the Romans. Not all Roman soldiers were Romans.

The centurion recognises authority – the authority of Rome, of Herod and of those above him, and the authority he has over 99 soldiers ranked below him. He recognises Jesus as *also* having authority, so he shows him respect, as an equal: 'You and I, Jesus, we understand authority. I have mine and you have yours. Please use yours to heal my servant.' Jesus had offered to come and heal him, but the centurion shows real faith and trusts there is no need. Yesterday we saw how Jesus touched the leper, breaking convention. In contrast Jesus offers to come and visit the sick, but is told that he, a healer, does not need to do this; his godly word is sufficient.

In the UK, medics were applauded during the Covid pandemic, and many died as a consequence of being in the proximity of those infected. Subsequently we saw the NHS struggling to deliver services, beset with resource issues, complaints and strike action. Patients said they could not get to see a doctor readily, if at all, while doctors struggled with heavy workloads. Consultations took place on the telephone – at a distance, with no visit to or from the surgery. Doctors say that in many cases they do not actually need to 'see' the patient to diagnose and treat illness.

The centurion is content with remote healing, having faith in Jesus to do it: faith grounded in hope, and rewarded in love.

Jesus, give me faith to trust in your loving power always. Amen.

GORDON GILES

Hand-holding

When Jesus entered Peter's house, he saw his mother-in-law lying in bed with a fever; he touched her hand, and the fever left her, and she got up and began to serve him. That evening they brought to him many who were possessed with demons, and he cast out the spirits with a word and cured all who were sick. This was to fulfill what had been spoken through the prophet Isaiah, 'He took our infirmities and bore our diseases.'

Peter, the founder of what is now known as the Roman Catholic Church, was married. In 284, two-and-a-half centuries later, Clement of Alexandria wrote that Peter had children, and there is a tradition that he had a daughter named Petronilla. Whether or not Petronilla existed, Peter's wife's mother certainly did, and she became unwell while Jesus was in town. It is possible to visit 'Peter's mother-in-law's house' in Capernaum to this day, and under a glass canopy lies the ruins of a building that could be exactly what it purports to be. We cannot be certain, but there is an air of authenticity to the whole neighbourhood; the synagogue ruins are nearby too.

Peter came from Bethsaida, two miles away. Perhaps he moved to Capernaum with his wife and her mother. Jesus heals her by touching her hand (this detail adds further authenticity), and she is restored to sufficient health to respond to his needs, he having responded to hers. There is an air of intimacy, for unlike all the others brought to him for healing, Jesus knows her, stays in her home and loves her, and the touch of the hand is an affectionate as well as healing gesture.

Think of those times in your life when you have touched or held hands. Young schoolchildren used to hold hands for security and safety. Couples hold hands when walking down the street; friends, colleagues and acquaintances shake hands. We had to learn not to during the pandemic. There is also the fundamentally human touch of reassurance that someone who is attending to someone in distress might touch or hold their hand. To take someone's hand is to communicate on a physical level, 'Don't worry, I am here and I care.'

Jesus, you are with me, you take my hand and you care. Amen.

GORDON GILES

Death and discipleship

A scribe then approached and said, 'Teacher, I will follow you wherever you go.' And Jesus said to him, 'Foxes have holes, and birds of the air have nests, but the Son of Man has nowhere to lay his head.' Another of his disciples said to him, 'Lord, first let me go and bury my father.' But Jesus said to him, 'Follow me, and let the dead bury their own dead.'

In the UK it can take a month or more to organise a funeral. There is much to do, and there is time to plan and prepare for the final opportunity to say farewell and thank you. By the time a funeral takes place, most of those present have begun to get used to the fact that someone has died, although the funeral itself brings the reality home. That does not make it any easier, necessarily, but British funerals, important as they are, are not organised in a way which makes them seem pressingly urgent.

Burying the dead in first-century Palestine, however, was an urgent task. In the story of Ananias and Sapphira (Acts 5:1–11), both bodies are taken out to be buried almost immediately. It is not only culturally acceptable but normal. Jewish and Islamic customs are more or less the same today.

The Old Testament made it clear that the dead need to be buried swiftly, and in hot climates it is obvious why: hygiene. This story presents the urgency of following Christ. It is not so much about breaking cultural rules or failing to do one's duty by the dead. Rather, it is about perspective and priorities, and the reference to the dead is not necessarily literal. It is about breaking the mould: foxes have holes and birds have nests, but that natural norm is not for Jesus and those who follow him. The more pressing task and concern of discipleship must instead take precedence.

That involves looking forward to new life, rather than being dragged down by the former, dead life that must be left behind. The old life is put to death, and those left behind with it can be the ones to bury it. Christ's call is to move onward towards resurrection life.

Jesus, help me to always look forward with you,
ever following in faith, hope and love. Amen.

GORDON GILES

Jesus onboard

When [Jesus] got into the boat, his disciples followed him. A windstorm suddenly arose on the sea, so great that the boat was being swamped by the waves, but he was asleep. And they went and woke him up, saying, 'Lord, save us! We are perishing!' And he said to them, 'Why are you afraid, you of little faith?' Then he got up and rebuked the winds and the sea, and there was a dead calm. They were amazed, saying, 'What sort of man is this, that even the winds and the sea obey him?'

There are two kinds of 'storm' – the kind where someone is in trouble, and the kind where there is a row (rather than a row!). The idea of a sudden storm whipping up in the Sea of Galilee, which often looks so calm, is frightening. These squalls were known and the dangers real – no doubt there were local stories about boats that had been caught up in such storms. Lake Tiberius, as it is also known, is exactly the same today.

Having Jesus on board, then as now, does not mean that the powers of nature are automatically overcome, nor that things do not get stormy. Storms happen – they just do – it is the way the planet is created, the way the universe works. Storms are part of the created order; they are not bad in themselves. Certain geological or meteorological conditions lead to them, and it is all part of the God-given freedom of the cosmos. So even with the Word made flesh in the boat, it still gets waterlogged and blown about.

This is why this terrifying story can be reassuring. For, strange as it may seem, this magical miracle is full of realism. On one level the calming of the storm is the biggest thing Jesus did – controlling the forces of nature, dictating to the single most powerful force on earth, the raging sea. Yet at the same time it speaks to us with a still, small voice, telling us that the commander of waves and winds is on board and on our side.

Heavenly Father, lead us over the world's tempestuous sea,
guard and guide us, for we have no help but you. Amen.

GORDON GILES

Preferring pigs

When [Jesus] came to the other side, to the region of the Gadarenes, two men possessed by demons came out of the tombs and met him… The demons begged him, 'If you cast us out, send us into the herd of swine.' And he said to them, 'Go!' So they came out and entered the swine; and suddenly, the whole herd stampeded down the steep bank into the sea and drowned in the water… Then the whole town came out to meet Jesus, and when they saw him, they begged him to leave their region.

One of the most interesting aspects of this vivid story is how it ends. Not simply with a herd of pigs imitating lemmings by hurling themselves into the lake, but rather with the delegation of townsfolk who ask Jesus to leave. As Gentiles they do not have the qualms about pork that other residents of the shores of the Sea of Galilee would have had. Elsewhere Jesus' actions might even have been welcomed, though Jesus does not have the herd run into the lake because he condemns pigs, nor because of their significant value.

Nevertheless, as the pigs rush into the sea, so too does the livelihood of their owners. In Thomas Hardy's novel *Far from the Madding Crowd*, the shepherd Gabriel Oak (whose very name reminds us of strength and kindness) is financially ruined when his young sheepdog chases his entire flock of sheep over a cliff into the sea. It may well be that the swineherds of Gadara were similarly ruined. They did not invite Jesus into their world to destroy their property and decimate their food supply. They prefer pigs to Jesus. Wealth, income and prosperity are more important than either divine power or the mental health of two local people. No wonder they asked him to leave!

Yet this is a miracle: an exorcism of not one but two demoniacs, tormented by demons who are so legion that they dement a whole herd. The locals do not appreciate it, but his disciples and we do. It shows great power and command over unruly supernatural powers, who themselves recognise and address Jesus as the Son of God.

Jesus, help us always to value you over anything else
we might possess or desire. Amen.

GORDON GILES

Holy and holistic

Some people were carrying to him a paralysed man lying on a stretcher. When Jesus saw their faith, he said to the paralytic, 'Take heart, child; your sins are forgiven.' Then some of the scribes said to themselves, 'This man is blaspheming.' But Jesus, perceiving their thoughts, said, 'Why do you think evil in your hearts? For which is easier: to say, "Your sins are forgiven," or to say, "Stand up and walk"?'

The connection between sickness and sin is primeval and persuasive. Even in our medically informed age we are aware of the relationships between physical health and well-being, spiritual and mental. Yet the landscape in which we view this story is vastly different to that of its time. It is easy to treat the opinion that sin affects health as primitive, but we know that mental well-being can have palpably physical affects, positive or negative.

In John's gospel, Jesus' disciples ask of a blind man, 'Who sinned, this man or his parents, that he was born blind?' (John 9:2; see 20 September). This view was prevalent. So when Jesus answers the Pharisees, his response is logical, but causes offence. The alternative – which they likely would have preferred – is that Jesus simply restore his health and leave sin out of it.

Jesus' approach is not only holy but also holistic. By pronouncing forgiveness of sins, he releases the man from physical restriction and mental torment. For the paralytic may have succumbed to Pharisaic spiritual conditioning: 'You are paralysed because you are a sinner.' Psychologically, sinners would be made to feel bad about themselves because they had a disability or illness. It could be a pernicious, cruel, hopeless and oppressive situation in which to be. Jesus confronts this disabling injustice and inevitably causes trouble, not only challenges the Pharisees' world view, but also undermines their spiritually abusive grip on the weak and helpless.

It is not so far removed from the ways in which spiritual abuse has been a rare but real facet of some Christians' lives in our own age too. Where the vulnerabilities of the physically or mentally weak are exploited, Jesus speaks and acts. So should we.

Christ our forgiver, bring your healing touch to all
who are damaged by sin. Amen.

GORDON GILES

Incisive power

'But so that you may know that the Son of Man has authority on earth to forgive sins' – he then said to the paralytic – 'Stand up, take your bed, and go to your home.' And he stood up and went to his home. When the crowds saw it, they were filled with awe, and they glorified God, who had given such authority to human beings.

Having confronted the manipulative connection between sin and disability, Jesus now acts with authoritative power. He transforms the link between sin and sickness into something positive: 'Because you are freed from the bonds of guilt and sin, you can walk. Get up and do so.' Jesus frees the man who now has no reason to be paralysed.

This transformative healing transcends the usual miracle-working that the bystanders and stretcher-bearers would have expected or hoped for. Some of them may have been sceptical – 'Let's see what he can do, if he can do anything at all.' One can imagine some 'healers' having a go and failing dismally.

Jesus is authentic and effective and they are not used to it. He also states unequivocally what he is doing and what it means. There is no room for doubt as the man gets up and leaves – released into a new world.

That Jesus has the authority and ability – as lamb of God – to take away the sins of the world is something that can be grounded in our world today. Readily overlooked or dismissed, it kicks in when we consider how many people are entangled with, even paralysed by, sinful behaviours which fuel a hidden and poisonous guilt, submerged on a deeper level than many can recognise. Jesus' response to the Pharisees is almost surgical in its incisive-ness. He cuts to the heart of the matter and exposes the abusive, coercive hypocrisy of the religious leaders, whose main objective is to protect the position of power they strive to protect and maintain. Yet it is Jesus who holds the true healing power, which he wields with divine authority to the benefit of those who suffer. It was an example to them and all, just as it is in our day.

Christ our King, heal and help your people
who cry out with sickness or shame. Amen.

GORDON GILES

Reality check-up

As Jesus was walking along, he saw a man called Matthew sitting at the tax-collection station, and he said to him, 'Follow me.' And he got up and followed him. And as he sat at dinner in the house… he said, 'Those who are well have no need of a physician, but those who are sick. Go and learn what this means, "I desire mercy, not sacrifice." For I have come to call not the righteous but sinners.'

Jesus says that only those who are sick need doctors, yet we all need medical care, and one of the greatest God-given gifts of medicine is the ability to predict and prevent, as well as cure, illness.

Occasionally I get invited by the surgery to have a check-up. Rather like spiritual direction, the encounter is both strange and familiar. Being weighed, having my blood pressure and cholesterol measured, and being quizzed about eating, drinking, smoking and exercise habits carries with it a whiff of 'judgement'. Some professions use the language of 'passing' a medical, and even though it is entirely optional, one wants a clean bill of health!

Yet it is a reality check. Often we are shown what we already know, and the purpose of these checks is salvation. Having a health snapshot signposts conditions and enables early intervention or detection. It also gives an opportunity to make changes for the good. This approach saves earthly lives. Also, it saves money. Sickness and serious medical conditions are expensive, so preventing them saves public money. Everyone is a winner.

Jesus' call to Matthew and his tax-collecting colleagues is an invitation to a spiritual health check, to change their lives and be saved. They need a doctor even though they do not know it. It is very easy to be sick and not know it. Cancers and heart diseases can lurk inside us, ready to take hold, or strike us suddenly, unseen, unpredicted. Perhaps like me, you have had dear friends and family struck down suddenly from heart attacks or fast-acting cancers. Yet Jesus did what the NHS now does: provide an opportunity to be examined such that flaws, weaknesses and dangerous habits can be illuminated, addressed and healed.

Jesus, examine us so that we, like Matthew,
may change our lives and be saved. Amen.

GORDON GILES

Lost children

A leader came in and knelt before him, saying, 'My daughter has just died, but come and lay your hand on her, and she will live.'… When Jesus came to the leader's house and saw the flute players and the crowd making a commotion, he said, 'Go away, for the girl is not dead but sleeping'… He went in and took her by the hand, and the girl got up.

As a flute player myself I note the reference here! Another reference to flutes in the gospels has Jesus quoting children: 'We played the flute for you, and you did not dance; we wailed, and you did not weep' (Luke 7:32). Here the flute players are reacting to the little girl's death. Mortality among children was common in the first century, but it was no less heart-breaking than nowadays. Recent research suggests that in Jesus' day half of children did not reach adulthood. In the UK today it is around one in a thousand. Nevertheless, charities like Abigail's Footsteps provide invaluable support for families who have lost children. Each year in mid-October, families come to Rochester Cathedral to see the west front lit blue and pink and to light candles. There are few words, and many tears. Only those who have lost children truly understand.

This story is not an easy one, therefore, for those whose children have died. Just as we saw with the leper and Peter's mother-in-law, Jesus takes the girl by the hand, defying religious and cultural convention, and hauls her back to life. Would that this were possible for so many who have seen their little ones suffer and die. Some of you, dear readers, will have 'been there' or known others who have. Jesus changes her story, but generally, history is not changed.

This miracle is not told to help us believe that people – of any age – do not die. Rather it serves to show that Jesus Christ, the Son of God, has authority not only over waves and wind, sickness and suffering, but also over life and death. Therefore, amid the traumas of loss of loved ones and the challenges of faith which they cause, there is hope: eternal hope.

God of love, hear the cries of all who grieve their little ones.
Grant them faith and hope. Amen.

GORDON GILES

Moving cure

Then suddenly a woman who had been suffering from a flow of blood for twelve years came up behind him and touched the fringe of his cloak, for she was saying to herself, 'If I only touch his cloak, I will be made well.' Jesus turned, and seeing her he said, 'Take heart, daughter; your faith has made you well.' And the woman was made well from that moment.

Matthew carefully intersperses this healing story with yesterday's story of the synagogue leader's daughter. In pulling them apart, I have deprived Matthew of some of his impact in connecting them. The whole of Matthew 9 is a case of 'one thing after another' – a flow of healings and questionings. There is no respite for the busy Jesus, trying to keep up with all the demands made upon him.

Christian ministry can seem like that: the tug on the sleeve; the 'I need to talk to you'; the person who stands close by when another conversation is going on, as if to say, 'I'm next.' Sometimes 'after-church coffee' can be like this for ministers. For many it is the only opportunity to catch up, have a word, relate some news, make an appointment, ask about a baptism or wedding or any other matter. Emails and phone calls are all very well, but there is no substitute for the 'facetime' of a conversation at church.

It is all done standing up. Recent research suggests that meetings done on one's feet are much more efficient, and this can be a technique for teaching: get the students or group to stand up to have quick two-minute discussions about something, and the results will likely be better, more focused and easier to assimilate than discussions held sitting down. Similarly, politicians 'work the room', moving from one person to the next, engaging with as many people as possible in a brief period.

This encounter takes place literally 'on the move' (as we saw yesterday, Jesus has an urgent destination). Although the poor woman has been seeking a cure for years, ultimately, with Jesus, it comes efficiently and instantly. Her faith, and her healing, is complete. In one sense it does not take much – simply a passing touch. Yet that little is everything.

Father, when we touch base with you amid the throng and press of life, make us whole again. Amen.

GORDON GILES

Eye-opening authenticity

As Jesus went on from there, two blind men followed him, crying loudly, 'Have mercy on us, Son of David!' When he entered the house, the blind men came to him, and Jesus said to them, 'Do you have faith that I can do this?' They said to him, 'Yes, Lord.' Then he touched their eyes and said, 'According to your faith, let it be done to you.' And their eyes were opened.

Thirty years ago, I visited a church in east London, at which, during a service a blind man was called forward. As the music swelled, the pastor laid his hands on him and told his eyes to be opened. He then asked if he could see. He said not. So he tried again, again to no avail. So he pushed the man away and said out loud, 'You don't have enough faith.' The blind man was abandoned to stumble back to his seat.

Then I was summoned, and the congregation was told that I was going to speak in tongues. Nothing was forthcoming, and I quietly told the pastor, at which he whispered, 'Pretend.' I returned to my seat at the back, to the overtones of some kind of evil spirit being cast out of me. The pastor was a charlatan, and while I was not particularly damaged by the experience, I remember it well decades later. In terms of modern church safeguarding language, I suppose it was a form of spiritual abuse, especially to the blind man.

The fact that there are people trying to emulate our Lord in these things, in his name, and encouraging others to be part of their act does not undermine the divine power of Jesus in such scenarios. Rather it emphasises his unique ability and power. In today's passage, the cooperation from the blind men is not coercive or collusive, but rather a simple verification: 'Do you have faith in my ability to do this?' They do.

I have faith in God to heal, but I did not have confidence in the manipulative pastor who was bringing attention to himself on that Sunday afternoon in east London. There is a huge difference. For it is not simply about the power of Jesus to heal, but the authenticity of the person. Jesus was both divinely powerful and authentic.

Thank you, Jesus, that you heal with authentic integrity. Amen.

GORDON GILES

An arsenal of mercy and love

After they had gone away, a demon-possessed man who was mute was brought to him. And when the demon had been cast out, the one who had been mute spoke, and the crowds were amazed and said, 'Never has anything like this been seen in Israel.' But the Pharisees were saying, 'By the ruler of the demons he casts out the demons.'

The healings continue as Jesus travels around the Sea of Galilee. This one is about speech rather than sight or paralysis, illness or even death. Not being able to speak is associated with demonic possession, but we know in our age that there are various potential explanations for muteness. Some people never develop speech, for physical or psychological reasons, and similarly some people lose the power of speech. Famously this happened to Zechariah, whose loss of speech during his wife Elizabeth's pregnancy can be thought of as prompted by a traumatic experience (Luke 1:20). Meanwhile some illnesses cause loss of speech: strokes, injuries, dementia and Parkinson's disease can steal speech from a sufferer. Medically this is known as aphasia or dysarthria. Perhaps more relevant to this story, epilepsy can cause speech loss, too, as can a variety of psychiatric conditions.

Jesus was demonstrably capable of curing not only diseases of the body, but also those of the mind. This story demonstrates another tool in his arsenal of mercy and love. As we are told, no one has ever seen anything like it. The range and precision of his healing power is wide and deep. Jesus is an all-rounder, for whom nothing is impossible. In this he is like God, because he *is* God.

As our world becomes increasingly aware of a great range of health issues and rightly develops a focus on well-being, we notice that Jesus knew this so long ago. He was releasing sufferers into better-being 2,000 years ago and, through the double action of prayer and medical practice, is at work today. Sickness is a spiritual as well as physical and mental issue, and whatever language we use to describe it, it is a truth universally acknowledged that mind, body and spirit are connected when it comes to pain, health and well-being.

We hold before you, Jesus, all who suffer in mind, body and spirit. Amen.

GORDON GILES

Counterpoint

Jesus went about all the cities and villages, teaching in their synagogues and proclaiming the good news of the kingdom and curing every disease and every sickness. When he saw the crowds, he had compassion for them because they were harassed and helpless, like sheep without a shepherd. Then he said to his disciples, 'The harvest is plentiful, but the labourers are few; therefore ask the Lord of the harvest to send out labourers into his harvest.'

When two musical lines are played together to create a blend of sound, it is called counterpoint. The two tunes weave their way independently, but are inextricably connected, even if one is silent briefly. They combine to sound in a unified yet distinguishably separate way. They work better together than alone, and each compliments and resonates with the mood, style and direction of the other. As two musical 'lines' they have mutual integrity, working together seamlessly and beautifully. J.S. Bach, who dedicated all his music 'to the glory of God', was a master of musical counterpoint.

These past two weeks we have seen the counterpoint of the kingdom of God revealed by Jesus. We have seen a symphony of healings, all revealing Jesus' authentic power, played out to us by Matthew. In each scenario Jesus taught and proclaimed the kingdom, not only alongside those deeds of power, but also *by* them. Actions can speak louder than words, perhaps, but we have seen that Jesus' actions and words are so connected that, whether or not we separate them, they sound together with mutual integrity.

The coming of the kingdom of God is revealed in signs and wonders: miracles of healing and exorcism. Such actions not only speak louder than words, they also *prove* the words. Some people are all talk; others are men or women of action. Jesus is both. His words and actions are intertwined in a counterpoint of the physical action and spiritual speech. In Jesus, uniquely, one cannot have one without the other. In his day, others could heal and others could teach, but only he could weave the counterpoint of teaching and healing which denotes the kingdom harvest which now begins.

Jesus, our redeemer, healer and friend,
sound the music of your kingdom in our hearts always. Amen.

GORDON GILES

The return of Christ

We are entering the season of Advent. For many the focus will be on preparing to celebrate the birth of Christ and on Christmas. However, another key theme of Advent is, or should be, the return of Christ. The church's response to this topic is decidedly mixed. There are some congregations where it has become a dominant emphasis. This can get out of hand, leading to all sorts of problems, and other important topics often get left out. Partly because of these excesses, many churches hardly look at the return of Christ from one year to the next. It is seen as a scary and difficult topic. We may say the Nicene Creed fairly frequently: 'He will come again in glory to judge the living and the dead, and his kingdom will have no end.' But do we really believe it? Even if we do, is it a lot easier to push it into a corner and forget about it?

We strongly believe that all Christians should have a firm understanding of the return of Christ. The Bible is very clear that it is an important area that demands our attention. It even has a whole vocabulary devoted to it! We will introduce and explain some of the terms in our reflections, but what we will cover is essentially what theologians call 'eschatology'. The *New International Dictionary of the Bible* says this includes, 'the second coming of Jesus Christ, the judgement of the world, the resurrection of the dead, and the creation of the new heaven and earth'. That sounds a bit heavy, and some of it certainly is. Yet it is an important subject to consider, and the idea that Jesus will return has sustained many Christians for the last 2,000 years.

In what follows we will investigate some of the key events, ideas and themes. Will we be able to tell when Jesus is going to return? What are the 'mechanics' of the return? What will the consequences be? How does the promised 'new heaven and new earth' play out in practice? Does it involve a destruction of the present order or a renewal of it? How should we live in the light of the impending return of Jesus? Join us as we try to find out!

MARGOT AND MARTIN HODSON

Coming on the clouds

'In my vision at night I looked, and there before me was one like a son of man, coming with the clouds of heaven. He approached the Ancient of Days and was led into his presence. He was given authority, glory and sovereign power; all nations and peoples of every language worshipped him. His dominion is an everlasting dominion that will not pass away, and his kingdom is one that will never be destroyed.'

Today is Advent Sunday, and if you go to church, you might sing the hymn 'Lo he comes with clouds descending'. The author is the great hymn-writer Charles Wesley (1707–88), who reworked an earlier Advent hymn by his friend John Cennick. The hymn quotes Revelation 1:7, which in turn quotes our reading for today.

As we sing the uplifting words of this hymn, we might ask: what are we expecting? Will Jesus literally come on clouds or does this passage describe something so awesome that it is impossible to put into words? Will there be a miracle so that we will all see him return together, or will we hear about it from others and have to decide if it is real? Will we be ecstatic, confused, frightened – or all those emotions together?

The first hearers of Daniel's dream might have been a bit perplexed. There are many places in the Bible where God is shown as riding on the clouds (e.g. Psalm 104:3). This image shows God's sovereignty. The nations around believed that a god of war, Baal, rode the clouds, but the psalmist makes it clear that it is the God of Israel, who is the only God. Who then could the 'son of man' be in Daniel 7? God, the Ancient of Days, has already arrived – who could be the one who comes and is given authority, glory and sovereign power? Many centuries later, the apostle, John, gives the answer in Revelation 1:7. The son of man riding on the clouds is the Lord Jesus. He rightfully takes his place alongside his heavenly Father.

We cannot know how this vision will be fulfilled, but we can trust that when Jesus returns, we will know and we will see him in glory.

Heavenly Father, Lord of the heavens, keep me looking for the return of your Son and guide us into all truth. Amen.

MARGOT HODSON

Going and coming

When he had said this, as they were watching, he was lifted up, and a cloud took him out of their sight. While he was going and they were gazing up toward heaven, suddenly two men in white robes stood by them. They said, 'Men of Galilee, why do you stand looking up toward heaven? This Jesus, who has been taken up from you into heaven, will come in the same way as you saw him go into heaven.'

Tragedies seem to be always in the news. It can be painful to watch as relatives and friends are exposed in the media at the height of their pain and bereavement. Their devastation is made so very public as their terrible loss is exposed.

I cannot imagine what it must have been like for the disciples in that fateful year of Jesus' death, resurrection and ascension. After the trauma of the crucifixion, one unexpected thing after another swept over them like waves. No wonder they were disoriented and wondered what would happen next. They believed Jesus to be the Messiah and expected him to restore the kingdom to Israel.

This was the question they asked him even as he prepared to return to the Father. Yet, instead of restoring Israel, he ascended from their sight. This was the final confusion – surely the Son of Man was supposed to descend on the clouds to judge the nations and declare his everlasting kingdom?

At the ascension, Jesus was exalted to the right hand of God and given authority and sovereign power. This was a fulfilment of the vision described in Daniel 7, which we read yesterday. Jesus has promised to return in the same way that he ascended, but meanwhile he has called us to be his 'witnesses in Jerusalem, and in all Judea and Samaria, and to the ends of the earth' (Acts 1:8). This might seem daunting, but these early chapters of Acts tell the story of Pentecost and the amazing promise that we have been, and will be, clothed with power from on high.

Whatever is happening in our lives at the moment, we can trust that the Holy Spirit is with us and we can ask him to work through us to make Christ's kingdom known in his world.

Lord, give us courage to step out in faith. Amen.

MARGOT HODSON

A thief in the night

Now, brothers and sisters, about times and dates we do not need to write to you, for you know very well that the day of the Lord will come like a thief in the night. While people are saying, 'Peace and safety', destruction will come on them suddenly, as labour pains on a pregnant woman, and they will not escape.

A long time ago, I spent a year working in Jerusalem. A friend of mine volunteered at Christ Church Hospice, a Christian hotel attached to the church just inside the Jaffa Gate. One day he was manning the reception desk when a new guest appeared to check in. My friend asked how long the new arrival wanted to stay. The response was somewhat surprising: 'Until Jesus returns, next Wednesday.' Wednesday came, and there was no sign of Jesus returning. This kind of occurrence was not that uncommon in Jerusalem.

People have been trying to predict the date of Christ's return since not long after Jesus' death and resurrection. Indeed, Paul told the Thessalonians not to be unsettled by those saying that it had already happened (2 Thessalonians 2:1–2). St Augustine thought that AD500 would be the date. Then, as the year 1000 approached, there was a great deal of expectation that Christ would return, but again nothing happened. More recently, Harold Camping, a Christian radio broadcaster, predicted it for both 1994 and 2011: again, nothing. One researcher catalogued about 300 of these predictions, and in every case they were wrong.

The phrase 'like a thief in the night' (v. 2) is one of those that has transferred from the Bible into popular culture, including in books, poems and songs – one even by the Rolling Stones! In most cases it is used to indicate a surprising event, and that is the way Paul intended it to be read. Despite all the predictions in the past 2,000 years, our scripture passage clearly states that Jesus' return will happen 'like a thief in the night'. It will be unexpected, and it will not be possible to calculate exact timings. You would be foolish to try.

'But about that day or hour no one knows, not even the angels in heaven, nor the Son, but only the Father' (Mark 13:32).

MARTIN HODSON

Patience

Be patient, therefore, beloved, until the coming of the Lord. The farmer waits for the precious crop from the earth, being patient with it until it receives the early and the late rains. You also must be patient. Strengthen your hearts, for the coming of the Lord is near. Brothers and sisters, do not grumble against one another, so that you may not be judged. See, the Judge is standing at the doors!

We live in a rural area, and in the winter many of the fields around us are bare. But we know that seeds are being sown. When the warmth of spring comes, the crops begin to germinate and flecks of green appear. As spring wears on these flecks become plants, and soon the fields are bright green before they flower and ripen. It seems a miracle, yet if you talk with the farmer, they will tell you of the work that has gone into growing the crop: preparing the soil, choosing a resistant crop for that soil and aspect of the field, keeping weeds and diseases at bay, plus the ever-present uncertainty of the weather. It takes patience and a fair bit of nerve. The investment is huge and can disappear in a single weather event.

Coming from rural Galilee, James understood the hard work, patience and courage that farmers need. He saw the tough years and anxiety when the rains failed to come. But he also saw the good years when the crops grew and ripened, giving a precious abundance at harvest.

James was writing to Christians who were facing difficulties and opposition. Like failing rain, they began to doubt their faith. So he reassures them that the coming of the Lord is near, and calls them to strengthen their hearts. In Hebrew thinking, the heart is not only a life-giving organ and the place where we feel emotions but is also the location of reason and decisions. When we strengthen our hearts, we are physically, emotionally and intellectually equipped to face whatever is to come.

We can start out with joyful and hopeful faith but as life wears on, the stresses and strains can leave our faith dry and faltering. We can take courage from James and strengthen our hearts, for the coming of the Lord is assured.

Lord, strengthen our hearts to have patience
and courage to wait for your return. Amen.

MARGOT HODSON

Wars and rumours of wars

Jesus answered: 'Watch out that no one deceives you. For many will come in my name, claiming, 'I am the Messiah,' and will deceive many. You will hear of wars and rumours of wars, but see to it that you are not alarmed. Such things must happen, but the end is still to come. Nation will rise against nation, and kingdom against kingdom. There will be famines and earthquakes in various places. All these are the beginning of birth-pains.'

We saw earlier in this series that there have been numerous attempts to calculate the date of the return of Christ, and all have proved to be incorrect. Nevertheless this does not mean that there will be no indications of when Jesus will return. In today's text, Jesus warns against false messiahs, and gives us some idea of what will happen just before he returns.

There were false messiahs even in the early days of the church. In Acts 5:34–39, Gamaliel, a Pharisee, spoke before the Jewish council to defend Peter and the apostles. He mentioned two false messiahs, Judas the Galilean and Theudas, who had risen to prominence and then rapidly faded away. He wisely advised the council that if Jesus was not the Messiah, then his movement would also die out; but if Jesus really was the Messiah, then nothing would stop the movement growing. We should expect more false messiahs before Jesus' return, and obviously they will deceive many people.

Jesus mentions three specific types of events, or 'signs of the times', which will precede his return: wars, famines and earthquakes. Yet there have been many such events in the last 2,000 years. Often when we experience major crises, people have suggested that a particular event was one of the signs. Thus the two world wars might have seemed to fit, but neither heralded the return of Jesus. Might it be that we should look for a particularly terrible event like a nuclear war, climate disaster or a whole series of such events? The truth is that we do not know. The only thing that is clear is that the return of Christ will happen at a time of global crisis.

'You know how to interpret the appearance of the sky,
but you cannot interpret the signs of the times' (Matthew 16:3).

MARTIN HODSON

One will be taken and the other left

'It will be just like this on the day the Son of Man is revealed… Whoever tries to keep their life will lose it, and whoever loses their life will preserve it. I tell you, on that night two people will be in one bed; one will be taken and the other left. Two women will be grinding corn together; one will be taken and the other left.'

Imagine one day you are walking and talking with a friend. You are in mid-sentence when suddenly your friend vanishes from sight! That is the kind of scenario depicted in the 'Left Behind' series of books and films, written by Tim LaHaye and Jerry B. Jenkins. The true Christians are taken away to heaven, leaving everyone else behind in an increasingly chaotic world. This event is known as the rapture and is based on a real theological idea.

Revelation 20:4 states that there will be a thousand-year reign of peace on earth, which has become known as the millennium. The type of theological system into which the rapture fits is known as premillennialism. Here Christians are taken to heaven immediately before a seven-year period of tribulation for those remaining on earth. After that period, Jesus returns with the church and begins the millennium before the last judgement happens. This thinking is popular with some Christian denominations, but many others think postmillennialism or amillennialism are a better fit with the Bible's words. Postmillennialism, popular in the 19th century, sees a thousand-year golden period during which Christianity expands before Jesus returns and the last judgement. Amillennialism, the most common position in UK denominations today, does not believe in a literal thousand years, but that we are already in a symbolic millennium, the age of the church. Once this age ends, Jesus will return and after the last judgement he will establish a permanent reign.

For 2,000 years theologians have argued about these viewpoints and come to very different conclusions. Whatever our view, we can be sure that Jesus will return, there will be judgement, the dead will be resurrected and the earth will be restored.

'A thousand years in your sight are like a day that has just gone by, or like a watch in the night' (Psalm 90:4). Amen.

MARTIN HODSON

Judgement

Enoch, the seventh from Adam, prophesied about them: 'See, the Lord is coming with thousands upon thousands of his holy ones to judge everyone, and to convict all of them of all the ungodly acts they have committed in their ungodliness, and of all the defiant words ungodly sinners have spoken against him.'

Nowadays judgement is not a popular theme, either inside or outside the church. We like to think of God as warm and friendly, but we are decidedly less sure about him bringing judgement. It is, however, clear that the return of Christ does involve a day of judgement, and we cannot get away from that. God's judgement is real.

Today's reading is unusual in that Jude quotes from 1 Enoch 1:9, a book in an ancient collection of texts called the Pseudepigrapha. Traditionally, the book is attributed to Enoch, the patriarch who was the great-grandfather of Noah. Modern scholarship suggests that the various sections date from 300BC to around the time of Christ. It is an apocalyptic book that is not considered as scripture by most Jewish and Christian authorities.

Even more strangely, 1 Enoch 1:9 is a Midrash (a Jewish textual interpretation) of Deuteronomy 33:2: 'The Lord came from Sinai and dawned over them from Seir; he shone forth from Mount Paran. He came with myriads of holy ones from the south, from his mountain slopes.' These kinds of complex allusions to obscure texts are difficult for us to understand, but we should remember that the first readers of Jude's epistle would have been very familiar with both Enoch and Deuteronomy.

Why does Jude use this extensive quote from Enoch with its hints of Deuteronomy? It is not definite, but I wonder if it was to emphasise his point. When I am writing scientific papers, I use direct quotes rarely and only to underscore an important argument. Was Jude using the same technique to make sure that his early readers understood that Christ's return involved judgement? Did it 'leap off the page' for them, yet is more hidden for us? Whatever is the case, we must all take the judgement of God seriously.

'For God will bring every deed into judgement, including every hidden thing, whether it is good or evil' (Ecclesiastes 12:14).

MARTIN HODSON

Burned up

But do not forget this one thing, dear friends: with the Lord a day is like a thousand years, and a thousand years are like a day. The Lord is not slow in keeping his promise, as some understand slowness. Instead he is patient with you, not wanting anyone to perish, but everyone to come to repentance. But the day of the Lord will come like a thief. The heavens will disappear with a roar; the elements will be destroyed by fire, and the earth and everything done in it will be laid bare.

On 19 July 2022, it was the hottest day Britain had ever seen. Temperatures topped 40°C (104°F) in places and an unexpected consequence was spontaneous fires. The ground was like a tinderbox and the slightest spark could turn into a full-blown catastrophe. Fire is horribly destructive. It can burn a crop within minutes, destroying homes and churches. All that is left is a bleak landscape.

Many biblical writers use fire as a metaphor for judgement. Here, Peter is explaining why Christians were still waiting for the Lord's return. God longs for people to repent and return to him. As in the time of Noah, he is waiting, but judgement will come. Judgement in Noah's day came with a devastating flood. Judgement in the 'day of the Lord' will be like a catastrophic fire. We cannot know how this will be, but the impact of the fire will be to lay bare the land. This passage does not say that the earth will be destroyed but, like the land at the time of Noah, it will be cleansed.

Something strange happens after a big fire. The ashes are rich in nutrients and plants spring up. Soon a blackened landscape can be a mass of colourful flowers. We cannot escape the fact that the coming of the Lord will bring judgement, but we must not forget the promise of salvation. Once the day of judgement is past, there will be new life.

Advent is an important time to examine our lives and put things right with God. Then we will be ready for whatever will come with the day of the Lord and have hope for the future beyond.

Lord, strengthen us for your future coming
and may we have courage to examine our lives before you. Amen.

MARGOT HODSON

Let them sing before the Lord

Shout for joy to the Lord, all the earth, burst into jubilant song with music… with trumpets and the blast of the ram's horn – shout for joy before the Lord, the King. Let the sea resound, and everything in it, the world, and all who live in it. Let the rivers clap their hands, let the mountains sing together for joy; let them sing before the Lord, for he comes to judge the earth. He will judge the world and the peoples with equity.

'Rewilding' is when land that we have changed for our own benefit is returned to the wild. Fields are allowed to grow into natural woodland, and animals, such as kites in England and bears in the Italian mountains, are reintroduced. Nature sings again.

If the weekend's passages seemed a bit scary, today's is the opposite. Why is the earth so joyful at the coming of the Lord to judge the world? It is tempting to look at the way humans have damaged the earth and wonder if the earth is hoping that it will at last see justice! But it is not that simple, because in restoring creation there is a role for redeemed humans. In Romans 8:19–22, Paul writes that creation is groaning and is waiting for the sons and daughters of God to be revealed. One day, all creation will be released from its bondage to decay and God's glory will be shown. The earth rejoices at our redemption and looks to us to release its praise.

It might be a surprise to discover that when we care for God's creation, we are pointing towards the return of Christ, when creation will be restored. When we care for wildlife by feeding birds, making our gardens hedgehog-friendly or joining a litter-pick in our local park, we are showing that we care for God's earth and look towards the time when Christ will return to restore it fully. Let us use Advent to see the nature around us with fresh eyes and give it reason to rejoice.

Lord, it pains us when we see your beautiful creation suffering
because of the damage that humans have inflicted on it.
Thank you that creation rejoices at your return,
and give us that same joy and fresh love for your world. Amen.

MARGOT HODSON

The Alpha and the Omega

'Look, he is coming with the clouds,' and 'every eye will see him, even those who pierced him'; and all peoples on earth 'will mourn because of him.' So shall it be! Amen. 'I am the Alpha and the Omega,' says the Lord God, 'who is, and who was, and who is to come, the Almighty.'

I love going 'behind the scenes' in the Bible. There is an obvious, and amazing, interpretation of 'the Alpha and the Omega' (v. 8). This certainly relates to Isaiah 44:6: 'This is what the Lord says – Israel's King and Redeemer, the Lord Almighty: "I am the first and I am the last; apart from me there is no God."' Later in Revelation (21:6; 22:13), the Alpha and the Omega is explained as the beginning and the end. From this, it is clear there is only one God, that Jesus is one of the Godhead, and that he is present at both the beginning and end of time.

But there is something even deeper going on here. There is an ancient rabbinical saying: 'The seal of God is truth.' The Hebrew word for truth is *emet*, with the spelling *aleph, mem, tav*. Interestingly, *aleph* is the first letter of the Hebrew alphabet, *mem* is the middle letter and *tav* is the last. The rabbis see *emet* as a word with special meaning. God is eternal and is there at the beginning, the middle and the end. So the Greek alpha and omega are the equivalent of *aleph* and *tav*. The early readers of Revelation would have recognised this. Moreover, *emet* has a wider meaning than just 'truth' (as against falsehood); 'trustworthiness' might be a better translation.

Paul picked up on this whole theme in Ephesians 1:13: 'And you also were included in Christ when you heard the message of truth, the gospel of your salvation. When you believed, you were marked in him with a seal, the promised Holy Spirit.' Note the relationship between truth and the seal. Then think of the 23 mentions of truth in John's gospel, far more than in any other book in the Bible. What is going on there? These are mind-blowing ideas, but every so often it does us all good to look a little deeper.

'I am the way and the truth and the life' (John 14:6).

MARTIN HODSON

The sign of the beast

The second beast was given power to give breath to the image of the first beast, so that the image could speak and cause all who refused to worship the image to be killed. It also forced all people, great and small, rich and poor, free and slave, to receive a mark on their right hands or on their foreheads, so that they could not buy or sell unless they had the mark, which is the name of the beast or the number of its name. This calls for wisdom. Let the person who has insight calculate the number of the beast, for it is the number of a man. That number is 666.

I once preached for 45 minutes on this passage at an evening service. I was fine, though, as our vicar spoke for over an hour at the previous week's service. He wanted an in-depth series on Revelation, and he certainly got it! I remember Margot reading the passage before my sermon, ending rather dramatically with 'Six. Six. Six.' The congregation was stunned.

Two questions stand out here. Who is the beast? And what does 666 mean? The beast is often identified as the Antichrist, a name which implies opposition to Christ, and is a false messiah, leading people astray. When I lived in Jerusalem, political figures such as Saddam Hussein and Mikhail Gorbachev were commonly suggested as the Antichrist, and as you might imagine certain present-day politicians have also been labelled in that way. This is nothing new – throughout history, political and religious leaders have frequently been named as the Antichrist. There is little doubt that people like Adolph Hitler had Antichrist-like attributes, but they cannot be *the* Antichrist, if we assume that the prophecies in Revelation can be taken in any way literally.

The number 666 is suggested to be *gematria*, a complex Hebrew code. Many commentators identify 666 as Caesar Nero. This would, of course, imply that the Antichrist was roughly contemporary with the writing of Revelation, which would suggest that it was not predicting events far into the future (the so-called preterist view). We should be very careful before we call someone the Antichrist, but Revelation gives us some clear ideas about the leaders that we should not follow.

Pray for world leaders, and for those who elect or select them.

MARTIN HODSON

A new heaven and a new earth

Then I saw 'a new heaven and a new earth,' for the first heaven and the first earth had passed away, and there was no longer any sea. I saw the Holy City, the new Jerusalem, coming down out of heaven from God, prepared as a bride beautifully dressed for her husband. And I heard a loud voice from the throne saying, 'Look! God's dwelling-place is now among the people, and he will dwell with them. They will be his people, and God himself will be with them and be their God.'

I remember a hymn in my childhood that begins, 'God has given us a book full of stories, which was made for his people of old; it begins with the tale of a garden and ends with the city of gold.' I always loved the idea of a garden but was rather worried by the idea of spending eternity in a city made entirely of gold. It was clearly going to be beautiful, but it felt a little cold and uncomfortable.

When we read Revelation, we find that the Bible ends with a far bigger and more exciting vision of the future. The city is there, but there is also a garden and a whole new heaven and earth. We have already read that Peter taught that the earth would be cleansed but not destroyed – so what does Revelation mean by a new heaven and earth? There are two words for 'new' in Greek that mean slightly different things: *neos* means completely new, but *kainos* means renewed or made new. I often joke that Martin and I have only ever had a *kainos* new car – it looks amazing and new to us when we buy it, but it has had a previous owner.

In this passage we have a *kainos* heaven and earth. God promises to renew his creation and restore it to the beautiful place that he always intended it to be. Far from sitting on gold chairs and drinking from gold cups, when we are in the new creation, we will be surrounded by creation's beauty, with God at the centre. We will be worshipping him, and maybe even gardening a little.

Lord, thank you for your wonderful promise of a new creation and help us to live lives that point towards it. Amen.

MARGOT HODSON

The healing of the nations

Then the angel showed me the river of the water of life, as clear as crystal, flowing from the throne of God and of the Lamb down the middle of the great street of the city. On each side of the river stood the tree of life, bearing twelve crops of fruit, yielding its fruit every month. And the leaves of the tree are for the healing of the nations.

I love trees, and I have been very fortunate to study a number of them. My first scientific paper was about a beech tree in mid-Wales, and so far I have published 16 more on various aspects of tree biology. The tree described in our passage today, the tree of life, will be fantastic to study, but I am hoping that I have a few more years yet before I get that opportunity!

Trees bookend the Bible. The tree of life first appears in Genesis 2:9, as does the tree of the knowledge of good and evil. The latter soon got humanity into all sorts of trouble, but the tree of life has much more positive connotations. Notably, similar trees appeared in Ezekiel's prophetic vision where freshwater flows from the temple in Jerusalem eastwards into the Dead Sea (Ezekiel 47:1–12). The trees in this vision also grow on either side of the river, and produce all kinds of fruit and leaves for healing. Both writers, John and Ezekiel, saw a time in the future when creation would be restored, there would be a super-abundance of produce, and the nations would be healed.

For over 30 years now, I have been working within the Christian environmental movement. In that period global environmental problems have steadily been getting worse. The church, for much of that period, showed little interest in these issues. But I am pleased to say that over the past five years or so the church's response has greatly improved. Witness the more than 6,000 churches in England and Wales that had signed up for the Eco Church scheme by summer 2023. At last, many churches are taking the environmental crisis seriously, and are helping with the healing and restoration that is so desperately needed.

'Creation is not confined for ever to its own immanent possibilities. It is open to the fresh creative possibilities of its Creator' (Richard Bauckham, The Theology of the Book of Revelation, Cambridge University Press 1993, p. 48).

MARTIN HODSON

Yes, I am coming soon

The Spirit and the bride say, 'Come!' And let the one who hears say, 'Come!' Let the one who is thirsty come; and let the one who wishes take the free gift of the water of life. I warn everyone who hears the words of the prophecy of this scroll: If anyone adds anything to them, God will add to that person the plagues described in this scroll. And if anyone takes words away from this scroll of prophecy, God will take away from that person any share in the tree of life and in the Holy City, which are described in this scroll. He who testifies to these things says, 'Yes, I am coming soon.' Amen. Come, Lord Jesus. The grace of the Lord Jesus be with God's people. Amen.

We arrive at the end of the book of Revelation and the scroll is sealed with a warning. We must neither add words to the book nor take them away – the prophecies must now be kept until Jesus returns. Most of the New Testament was written on 'codexes' – these were small sheets made of wood or other fibres and were more commonly used for lists of merchandise and other commerce. A codex was less cumbersome than a scroll but was also seen as less enduring. A scroll had more permanence and that is emphasised here. However, it is not the scroll or codex that is important, it is the message it contains.

In this series we have grappled with some challenging concepts in seeking to understand the return of Christ, and we realise that there will be trials ahead. Some passages are difficult to understand, and we will not know what they mean until the future unfolds – whenever that will be. One thing we can be certain of: at the heart of the book of Revelation is an invitation, 'Come'! We call on Christ to return and Christ calls us to come and enter into his grace. Amid all the trials and tribulations of Revelation, we can trust the central message that Jesus will return and we are invited to abide in him forever.

If you are thirsty for a deeper relationship with Christ, if you are longing to have a greater reality of faith, then Christ's message is simple: 'Come.'

MARGOT HODSON

The O Antiphons

The O Antiphons are ancient prayers: they were already in use by the seventh century and are probably older than that. The seven prayers herald the advent of Jesus by recalling images and names used in Old Testament prophecies about the Messiah. Each prayer calls out to Jesus using one of those titles, beginning with the word 'O'. They are sometimes called the Great Os.

Originally in Latin, the O Antiphons are astonishingly rich and dense pieces of poetry, cramming several scriptural references into just a few lines. Since those very early days, they have been chanted or prayed daily from 17 to 23 December, and although the prayers themselves are no longer heard in every church, they survive in the Advent hymn 'O Come, O Come Emmanuel'.

The O Antiphons place us imaginatively at a time before Jesus. The prophets, trusting in God's promises, provided pictures of what the coming Christ would be like. For every picture of the Messiah, there is a picture of humanity in need of salvation, waiting and longing for rescue. For the people dwelling in darkness, there is a light; for the prisoners, a key; in the confused chaos of the fallen world, wisdom which puts everything in order. As we pray through the 'Great Os', we consider the change Jesus' birth brought to history and our own need for a saviour. Calling him by these prophetic, Old Testament names, we remember his first coming and ask him to return as he promised.

The prayers move through the final week of Advent in the order of the gospel story, taking us from creation, through God's people in the wilderness and the promised land and finishing with Emmanuel, 'God with us'. Reading them daily, we arrive at Christmas having been reminded of God's eternal promises, and with a renewed thankfulness for the long-awaited miracle of the incarnation.

I have provided each O Antiphon as the prayer for the day on which it falls. Before they begin, we will look at Zechariah's song from Luke 1, which echoes many of the Antiphons' themes.

AMY SCOTT ROBINSON

The promise of God's presence

'Thus he has shown the mercy promised to our ancestors, and has remembered his holy covenant, the oath that he swore to our ancestor Abraham, to grant us that we, being rescued from the hands of our enemies, might serve him without fear, in holiness and righteousness in his presence all our days.'

Luke's gospel opens with an angel announcing a miraculous birth, but it is not the birth of Jesus. Instead, Luke begins with John the Baptist, who would grow up to baptise Jesus and to herald the beginning of his ministry. John's father, Zechariah, is made temporarily mute when he disbelieves the angelic messenger. Once he can speak again, he sings this prophetic song over his new son.

The song seems to come from the Old Testament, while standing on the brink of the New. Zechariah looks back to God's covenant with his people, beginning with Abraham, and claims that it is now being fulfilled. The way he names God's promises reads like a summary of the prophets and reflects many of the images picked up in the O Antiphons.

He begins with an image of rescue and the freedom to serve without fear in the presence of God. It is not just that people will no longer fear their enemies, but that the presence of God will become peaceful rather than terrifying. For Zechariah, whose last encounter in God's sanctuary involved being struck dumb by an angel, that is quite a claim.

Even though he served as a priest in the temple, and had even experienced the rare privilege of entering the sanctuary, Zechariah's longing to be in God's presence is palpable. He can think of nothing better than to serve in holiness and righteousness all the days of his life, and he senses that someone is coming who can somehow make that fearless service a reality.

Zechariah's song, like the O Antiphons, puts us in the mindset of people who could not have imagined the end of God's plan. Do you ever stop and think how extraordinary it is just to approach God daily without fear?

Lord, we are looking for you, waiting for you, longing to be with you.
Come to us, so that we may be fearless in your presence,
serving you forever. Amen.

AMY SCOTT ROBINSON

Familiar phrases

'Because of the tender mercy of our God, the dawn from on high will break upon us, to shine upon those who sit in darkness and in the shadow of death, to guide our feet into the way of peace.'

In our college chapel, we had an adventurous organist with a cheeky sense of humour. If you listened carefully enough to her voluntaries, you could hear her sneaking in snatches of popular songs and contemporary film themes – I remember Star Wars and Harry Potter making frequent appearances! Reading Zechariah's song is a bit like that. How many Old Testament passages are echoed in this brief excerpt? There's certainly some Isaiah 9 and perhaps a bit of Psalms 23 and 119:105, and that is just in the last two lines.

Just as our organist was familiar with her music, reproducing it on a whim, so Zechariah knew scripture. It flowed through him, so that in this moment of prophecy, the Holy Spirit was able to bring out those familiar phrases and recombine them into a new song about how God's promises were being fulfilled. The people listening to him, if they had the same understanding, would have recognised those words and images and known the stories and the people that they recalled. This new prophecy was firmly rooted in what had gone before.

We will see over the next few days that the writer of the O Antiphons had a similar grasp of the Bible, and as we read them, we will look for those echoes too.

You might have a solid routine for reading the Bible, and an excellent memory for chapter and verse; or perhaps you are more like me, with erratic quiet-time habits and an over-reliance on Google. Whichever it is, let us pick up our Bibles as much as we can, absorbing scripture as poetry, inspiration, history and instruction: not just so that we can recognise its echoes in passages like this, but so that it fills us, nourishes us and starts to flow back out again in prayer as God's words to his world.

God, you have given us your rich, powerful and beautiful word.
May we rejoice in reading and hearing it, and may its echoes
repeat through our daily lives. Amen.

AMY SCOTT ROBINSON

O Sapientia (O Wisdom)

When he established the heavens, I was there; when he drew a circle on the face of the deep, when he made firm the skies above, when he established the fountains of the deep, when he assigned to the sea its limit… then I was beside him, like a master worker, and I was daily his delight, playing before him always, playing in his inhabited world and delighting in the human race.

In Proverbs 8, personified Wisdom speaks and recalls the unfolding of creation. She says that she was the first of the acts of creation, there before the beginning of the earth, and from this we can understand that all creation comes from God's wisdom, making it entirely good and right. In verse 8, Wisdom says that all the words of her mouth are righteous, and 'there is nothing twisted or crooked in them'. Anything that proceeds from God's wisdom is perfect.

In Wisdom's description of creation (vv. 27–29), we see the skies separated from the waters, the boundaries of the seas marked out, and the foundations of the earth set in place. From the heavens to the deep, nothing is out of God's reach, and yet everything has its place and its limit: the waters are not allowed to disobey God's command. God's wisdom puts everything in order and holds it in check. It is a picture of solidity and safety.

That is why verse 30 is such a delightful surprise. God and Wisdom play together as the earth takes shape, and delight in the new human race. The word translated as 'playing' has the sense of laughter: there is an almost childish pleasure in the result of those wise boundaries and safe limits. Wisdom goes from looking like a careful architect to resembling a joyful toddler, secure in the love and protection of her parent; in fact, some translations offer 'little child' as an alternative to 'master worker' (v. 30).

This is the Wisdom that the first O Antiphon calls: the one who encompasses everything, puts all our chaos in order, and gives us the freedom to rejoice and delight in safety and security. That is the way of prudence.

O Wisdom, which came out of the mouth of the Most High,
and reaches from one end to another, mightily and sweetly
ordering all things: come and teach us the way of prudence.

AMY SCOTT ROBINSON

O Adonai (O Lord)

Moses said, 'I must turn aside and look at this great sight and see why the bush is not burned up.' When the Lord saw that he had turned aside to see, God called to him out of the bush, 'Moses, Moses!' And he said, 'Here I am.' Then he said, 'Come no closer! Remove the sandals from your feet, for the place on which you are standing is holy ground.' He said further, 'I am the God of your father, the God of Abraham, the God of Isaac, and the God of Jacob.' And Moses hid his face, for he was afraid to look at God.

The name Adonai, often rendered 'Lord' in the Bible, sometimes in capitals, was written to avoid having to write the holy name of God; and when God appears in the text as YHWH, the name Adonai was read aloud instead. It is a reverent substitute for a name too holy to say.

The thing that fascinated Moses about the burning bush was that the bush itself was not being destroyed by the fire. Moses would have expected consuming fire from God. The surprise was that nothing was consumed. God revealed himself to Moses as merciful, choosing to redeem and protect instead of destroy.

Just as the name Adonai allows a human being to speak of God without naming him, so Moses took off his sandals and hid his face. An encounter with God made the ground holy; looking at God could mean death. This is the fearful reaction we see from many Old Testament characters who met the Angel of the Lord.

For a human to meet with God, it was God who had to draw near. God had to hold back the fire from consuming, and warn Moses not to come closer. What a contrast with the vulnerable baby who arrived in Bethlehem. When we call 'Adonai' in the second O Antiphon, we remember the unimaginably holy and powerful Lord God who chose to preserve and redeem us when we expected destruction.

O Adonai, and leader of the house of Israel, who appeared in the bush to Moses in a flame of fire, and gave him the Law in Sinai:
come and deliver us with an outstretched arm.

AMY SCOTT ROBINSON

O Radix Jesse (O Root of Jesse)

A shoot shall come out from the stump of Jesse, and a branch shall grow out of his roots. The spirit of the Lord shall rest on him, the spirit of wisdom and understanding, the spirit of counsel and might, the spirit of knowledge and the fear of the Lord... On that day the root of Jesse shall stand as a signal to the peoples; the nations shall inquire of him, and his dwelling shall be glorious.

Isaiah 10 finishes with a picture of God hacking down a forest with an axe, so the image that opens chapter 11 is not just of a single stump, but a destroyed forest. Isaiah was writing about the destruction that was coming to Israel through Assyria. The scene is one of overwhelming loss.

But then, a tiny movement catches the eye. Have you ever seen a time-lapse video of a plant growing? Isaiah describes a small shoot, then a branch growing from one of the tree stumps. It is the stump of Jesse, father of King David: cut down so far that the royalty has been cut off. But this new branch will become a king of all nations, full of the Holy Spirit. This king is a picture of new life and hope: a promise that God still has a future plan, even in the midst of destruction.

After describing a beautiful picture of the redeemed earth under the reign of this king, Isaiah imagines a tree from that root standing tall as a signal to all nations. This king has a glorious dwelling, so visible that the scattered people of God can see him and come to rejoin the kingdom of God.

Isaiah will return to this image in 52:13–15, with a servant lifted up 'very high' so that 'kings shall shut their mouths', but here there is an extra detail: his appearance is marred 'beyond human semblance'. Here the glorious tree gives way to a foretaste of the cross, a sign to all people that it is now possible to return to God.

O Root of Jesse, which stands as an ensign of the people,
at whom kings shall shut their mouths, whom the gentiles seek:
come and deliver us, and do not delay.

AMY SCOTT ROBINSON

O Clavis David (O Key of David)

These are the words of the Holy One, the True One, who has the key of David, who opens and no one will shut, who shuts and no one opens: 'I know your works. Look, I have set before you an open door, which no one is able to shut.'

The voice of Jesus in this verse from Revelation quotes directly from Isaiah 22:22. Like so many of Isaiah's prophecies, it had both a contemporary and a Messianic meaning. Isaiah was writing about a transfer of authority within the royal household: whoever has the keys to the household has the final say on which parts of the house are accessible to others. Jesus applies that authority to himself, and holds the keys not just to a house, but to heaven and earth. He takes the picture one step further with the image of an open door that nobody can shut.

The writer of the Antiphons has found an echo here of another moment when Jesus applied Isaiah's words to himself. In the synagogue at the beginning of his ministry, Jesus read a passage about proclaiming release to captives and to the oppressed, and said, 'Today this scripture has been fulfilled in your hearing' (Luke 4:16–21). The people listening in the temple may have heard that passage as referring to the oppression of Israel by Rome, and hoped for a Messiah to release them. Perhaps today, we think of literal prisoners and oppressed peoples. We know God is against oppression. Jesus, however, was thinking further ahead.

Jesus' death opened a door out of sin for humanity to approach God, symbolised by the curtain in the temple being torn in two, opening the holiest place. A door stands open in the division between earth and heaven, people and God. Jesus' resurrection opened the door between death and life, and kept that door open too. In this image, we are the prisoners waiting in the darkness, and Christ is the key to freedom, light and life.

---

*O Key of David and Sceptre of the house of Israel; that opens,
and no one shuts, and closes, and no one opens:
come and bring the prisoner out of the prison,
and them that sit in darkness and the shadow of death.*

AMY SCOTT ROBINSON

O Oriens (O Rising Sun)

But for you who revere my name the sun of righteousness shall rise, with healing in its wings. You shall go out leaping like calves from the stall.

The Latin word *Oriens* is tricky to translate. It appears as Dayspring, Morning Star, Dawn, Guiding Light. It has the sense both of a light that appears in the morning, and that same light orienting us – because, of course, that is where the word 'orient' comes from. We know that the sun rises in the east, and so at daybreak we know which way we are facing. For travellers in the desert or on the sea, dawn is a daily course corrector and reassurance that they have been going the right way.

Malachi observes the effect of the rising sun on animals, with his picture of calves leaping out of the stall towards pasture, their joy and energy on full show after a night of confinement. Like the prisoners in yesterday's Antiphon, this is a picture of release.

There is still more than that in Malachi's poetry. His rising sun is the sun of righteousness: as if it has been night for as long as sinfulness has been a part of humanity, but now, at last, a new, sinless day is dawning. The sun rises 'with healing in its wings'. Earth's long night comes to an end, and the dawn brings healing from all the consequences of sin, the greatest of which is death. No wonder we will be leaping about like calves greeting the sunshine.

In today's Antiphon, the Latin word *illumina*, here cleverly translated as 'enlighten', also has a double meaning. Those dwelling in darkness are illuminated, enlightened with a fresh understanding. In the light, we can clearly see things which were dim or invisible in the dark: the ogre in the corner of the bedroom is just a crumpled dressing gown. The truth is revealed.

When we call Christ 'Oriens', we ask him to show us the way, release us, heal us, fill us with joy and give us new, clear knowledge of his kingdom.

O Dayspring, Brightness of Light Everlasting, and Sun of Righteousness: come and enlighten them that sit in darkness and the shadow of death.

AMY SCOTT ROBINSON

O Rex Gentium (O King of the Nations)

'Thus says the Lord God: I will take the people of Israel from the nations among which they have gone and will gather them from every quarter and bring them to their own land. I will make them one nation in the land, on the mountains of Israel, and one king shall be king over them all. Never again shall they be two nations, and never again shall they be divided into two kingdoms.'

In today's O Antiphon, although the title being addressed is 'king of the nations', the main picture is of a cornerstone, where two walls join together. It reminds me of this passage from Ezekiel. Ezekiel has been told to take two sticks, write 'Joseph' on one and 'Judah' on the other, and join them together to show the two opposing kingdoms of Israel becoming one again. He goes on to prophesy that God will bring his scattered people from all the nations, and make them one nation under one king.

This echoes the beautiful image in Isaiah 2 of people from every nation streaming uphill, like a reversed river, to put themselves under the instruction of God in his house. In both passages, a mountain is part of the image: a high place that attracts people towards it and unites them. God's kingdom is attractive, and his rule is irresistible. In contrast with earthly kings, he does not need to conquer and oppress to grow his kingdom; instead, people simply flow towards it and unite in peace, all ancient quarrels and wars behind them.

At the beginning of the story of the Bible, the entrance of sin into God's perfect world had two results: people were separated from people (Adam and Eve blaming each other; Cain trudging away into exile; the nations split apart at Babel) and people were separated from God. The aim of God's salvation throughout the Bible is twofold: to join people together, and to join humanity back to himself. The closer we go to God, the closer we come to each other, and Jesus, king of the nations, unites us in peace.

O King of the Nations, and their Desire; the Cornerstone, who makes both one: come and save humankind, whom you formed from clay.

AMY SCOTT ROBINSON

O Emmanuel

For a child has been born for us, a son given to us; authority rests upon his shoulders, and he is named Wonderful Counsellor, Mighty God, Everlasting Father, Prince of Peace. Great will be his authority, and there shall be endless peace for the throne of David and his kingdom. He will establish and uphold it with justice and with righteousness from this time onward and forevermore. The zeal of the Lord of hosts will do this.

Isaiah first coined the name Emmanuel, which means 'God With Us', a couple of chapters before this: but here we see the full picture of a child, born for us, who is named Mighty God. In this passage, the pictures from all the O Antiphons come together.

This child has authority linked to the throne of David, as echoed in the Root of Jesse and the Key of David. He is called Wonderful Counsellor, like the Antiphons' title of Wisdom, and Mighty God, like Adonai. The passage begins, in Isaiah 9:2, with people who walked in darkness seeing a great light, echoed in the O Rising Sun prayer. It finishes with a righteous king ruling over a peaceful kingdom for ever, as we saw in O King of the Nations.

As Isaiah points out at the end of verse 7, 'the zeal of the Lord of hosts will do this'. This peaceful kingdom of enlightened people cannot take place on human terms. In each of the pictures we have looked at, humanity is helpless. We need wisdom to order our chaos, a key to free us from our prison, light to guide us from our darkness. By placing ourselves into these pictures of people in need of a saviour, it becomes clear: the greatest need of the human race is to have God with us.

I wonder, as Isaiah wrote this passage which, to us, so clearly refers to Jesus, how he would have imagined his prophecy coming true. If he could have seen 700 years into the future to the birth and life of Jesus, would he have been surprised? We are going to dwell imaginatively with him in the Old Testament for one more day, because the O Antiphons hold one last, wonderful surprise, as we shall see on Christmas Eve.

O Emmanuel, our King and Lawgiver, the Desire of all nations,
and their Salvation: come and save us, O Lord our God.

AMY SCOTT ROBINSON

ERO CRAS

'It is I, Jesus, who sent my angel to you with this testimony for the churches. I am the root and the descendant of David, the bright morning star'… The one who testifies to these things says, 'Surely I am coming soon.' Amen. Come, Lord Jesus!

The writer of the O Antiphons wrote seven different prayers to Jesus, addressing him by seven different titles and calling him seven times to come and save his people. But as that anonymous person wrote these chants, they slipped in a hidden surprise: the answer.

If, on Christmas Eve, you look back through all the O Antiphons and take the first letter of each Latin name in reverse – starting with Emmanuel and going back to Sapientia – it spells the Latin phrase '*ERO CRAS*', which means 'I am coming – tomorrow!'

I love the fact that this unknown writer or writers, standing imaginatively with all those who lived before Christ, putting the longing of all humanity into words, knew that Jesus hears and answers our call. Just as God knew the needs of his people, and answered their pleas for salvation by coming into the world at the first Christmas, so the whole Bible finishes with Jesus' promise: he will come again. He is coming soon. The everlasting reign of peace that he promised is still on the way.

And while we wait, in the chaos, darkness and oppression which is often so much a part of our world and our lives, our continued prayers and longing for him always contain his loving answer. On this side of the first Christmas, we do know the rest of the story. We know that Christ's death and resurrection have saved us and given us hope of eternal life with him, whatever else comes in between. Whenever we call out to him, we can believe his reply: 'I'm on my way.'

Amen. Come, Lord Jesus!

Lord, as we stand on the brink of Christmas, we thank you that you are just around the corner. Thank you for being our wisdom, our Lord, our new life; the open door from our prison, the guiding light in our darkness, our everlasting king. Come and be with us always. Amen.

AMY SCOTT ROBINSON

If you've enjoyed this set of reflections by **Amy Scott Robinson**, check out her books published with BRF Ministries…

Images of the Invisible
Daily Bible readings from Advent to Epiphany

978 0 85746 789 8
£8.99

Images of Grace
A journey from darkness to light at Easter

978 1 80039 117 8
£9.99

To order, visit **brfonline.org.uk** or use the order form at the end.

Bethlehem

Editor's note: As this issue went to press, the situation in the Holy Land had become of increasing concern globally. We are distressed at what has occurred in that region since these reflections were written, and our focus is on peace, reconciliation and compassion for there and across the world.

The nearest I ever got to Bethlehem was my passage down the Suez Canal by emigrant ship! However, even a stopover in Aden gave a little flavour of the Middle East, which we may fail to catch when we are reading our Bibles. The sheer poverty of the whitewashed, mudbrick houses; people sleeping rough in the streets without mattress or covering; animals wandering about freely and seemingly unfed – this is the reality of subsistence life today. Would it have been any better in Bethlehem at the time of Augustus' census, particularly with the overcrowding that would have occurred as a result?

Bethlehem's history is a sad one. It starts life as a cemetery, only brightening as time goes on. There is controversy about its foundation, and the town's story includes one particularly sad and regrettable episode. Its story brightens with David's birth and Ruth's story, eventually becoming unforgettable in the New Testament narratives of Matthew and particularly Luke, who makes a political point against the authorities by giving Bethlehem the title 'city of David', a name usually given only to Jerusalem!

We are going to follow the evolving history of this little town as we draw near to and pass through yet another Christmas. We can, I hope, even afford to think about something beyond the Christmas of long ago to the Christ-feast that lies ahead of us – that future time which we should have been thinking about with joyful anticipation right through Advent – not allowing the build-up to Christmas day to get in the way!

For most, with all the festivity, there may not be time for a *New Daylight* reading, but you might be able to catch up! Others may feel they have all too much time! Whichever is you, spare a thought for the loneliness of a young pregnant teenage fiancée, finding herself in a strange and apparently unfriendly town where there is no suitable accommodation available, forced to give birth in a cowshed. The most solitary among you might be able to feel that you are in very good company.

PAUL GRAVELLE

The king is coming

The Lord says, 'Bethlehem Ephrathah, you are one of the smallest towns in Judah, but out of you I will bring a ruler for Israel, whose family line goes back to ancient times.' So the Lord will abandon his people to their enemies until the woman who is to give birth has her son... When he comes, he will rule his people with the strength that comes from the Lord and with the majesty of the Lord God himself. His people will live in safety because people all over the earth will acknowledge his greatness, and he will bring peace.

With Margot and Martin Hodson's and Amy Scott Robinson's reflections, we have been encouraged to look forward to the future coming of our Saviour throughout the Advent season, and not allowed ourselves to look back to much at his first Advent, which we are honouring today.

Today's reading is one of the great Messianic prophecies which looks forward to both the appearing of Jesus as the Jewish Messiah and his future appearing as universal King. What a wonderful scripture for Christmas Day! I unashamedly love prophecies which encourage me to look forward to the future like this. Do you?

Tom Wright, one of the greatest theologians of our day, encourages us to rid ourselves of the medieval idea of going to heaven when we die and to work for the kingdom of God which Jesus will establish on earth when he returns. His book *Broken Signposts* (HarperCollins, 2020) develops this theme wonderfully. He takes his readers through John's gospel, showing how Jesus' interpretations of justice, beauty, love and four other themes turn them into signposts for making sense of this world while we remain in it.

It is all too easy to slip into the popular view that we escape to live somewhere beyond this world when this life is over. The Bible points us to a different scenario. It shows that we will join Jesus here, when he returns to earth. That is a wonderfully reassuring promise – a Christmas gift for anyone who wants to receive it!

Christmas blessings to you, wherever you are.

Glory to God in the highest heaven, and peace on earth
to those with whom he is pleased. Amen.

PAUL GRAVELLE

Place of burial

Jacob and his family left Bethel… The time came for Rachel to have her baby, and she was having difficult labour… She was dying, and as she breathed her last, she named her son Benoni, but his father named him Benjamin. When Rachel died, she was buried beside the road to Ephrath, now known as Bethlehem. Jacob set up a memorial stone there, and it still marks Rachel's grave to this day.

Who wants to be thinking about burial grounds on Boxing Day? No jokes about 'boxes', please. On the other hand, if you have experienced a hard time preparing for the festivities in the days leading up to Christmas, you might just want to crawl away and hide now that it is all over. That would be a kind of burial, would it not?

Originally, long before Caleb, Bethlehem seems to have begun its time as a place to have been avoided rather than a permanent resting place – except for the dead! We first read about Bethlehem as a burial ground. Jacob chose Ephrath as the place to bury his favourite wife Rachel, and later we read that one of the judges, Ibzan, was also buried there. Later still, David's champion, Asahel, was also buried at Bethlehem.

There is something that we should not forget at this season, which is that the baby over whom we rejoice and sing carols about at our Christmas services was destined for a grave. Unlike Rachel, however, he was to rise again and demonstrate the truth of his promise of eternal life. For Christians there is always a big focus on the cross. This worries me sometimes because the cross without the resurrection is a symbol of death, and death without any resurrection is hopeless! Paul wrote this to the Corinthians: 'If our hope in Christ is good for this life only and no more, then we deserve more pity than anyone else in all the world' (1 Corinthians 15:19).

Lord, we rejoice in your birth, death, resurrection and everything
in between – all that we know about your amazing visit to us
here on this earth which you created for us to live on. Thank you
that you are coming again to bring your resurrection life to us. Amen.

PAUL GRAVELLE

Sad stories

Micah had his own place of worship. He made some idols and an ephod, and appointed one of his sons as his priest. There was no king in Israel at that time; everyone did whatever they wanted. At that same time there was a young Levite who had been living in the town of Bethlehem in Judah. He left Bethlehem to find another place to live... Micah said, 'Stay with me. Be my adviser and priest, and I will give you ten pieces of silver a year, some clothes and your food.'

This is the beginning of some very sad stories which centre around Bethlehem. They continue through Judges 17—19. The upshot of these tales is that it looks as if it would have been better if the young Levite had stayed in Bethlehem! It is not clear whether there are two Levites involved or just the one, but the consequence of wandering away is greed, envy, violence, theft and eventually rape and murder.

Perhaps we should look on these sad tales – which you may want to read, if you have not already – as parables. They are about the dangers of wandering away from a safe place into foreign parts where there will be strong temptations to try lifestyles which seem to be fine at first but which eventually turn out to be disastrous.

Even in these questionable and sometimes horrific situations, Bethlehem is seen as the safe home to which it is always possible to return. Similarly, years later when the holy family arrived, Bethlehem was a safe place where shelter was to be found. I am always happy to see that by the time the magi appear, they find Mary and Joseph comfortably housed: 'They went into the house, and when they saw the child with his mother Mary, they knelt down and worshipped him' (Matthew 2:11a).

Even if we have wandered away from what we know is the way that Jesus wants us to follow, now is the ideal time to turn and go back to Bethlehem – where we can always find him again.

Thank you, Jesus, that you are a safe home
to whom we can always return and find welcome. Amen.

PAUL GRAVELLE

Place of wonderful outcome

They went on until they came to Bethlehem. When they arrived, the whole town became excited, and the women there exclaimed, 'Is this really Naomi?' 'Don't call me Naomi,' she answered... 'When I left here, I had plenty, but the Lord has brought me back without a thing...' This, then, was how Naomi came back from Moab with Ruth, her Moabite daughter-in-law. When they arrived in Bethlehem, the barley harvest was just beginning.

Can you sense the excitement in this last phrase, 'the barley harvest was just beginning'? Perhaps the phrasing might have provided a bit more of the fairy-tale atmosphere which I can sense! For the story of Ruth is about her being discovered by the handsome landowner Boaz, who eventually takes her under his wing and marries her. We know that Bethlehem was the centre of a rich farming district, so he would have been much sought-after as a husband. But he chose this destitute immigrant as his bride. It is the stuff of fairy tales, and it all takes place in Bethlehem!

We do not, though, hear anything exciting about Orpah, Naomi's other daughter-in-law, also widowed. It is not really a fairy tale; it is a real-life tale. And it is there in the Bible because God was in it. God is not mentioned once in the little book of Ruth, but you can see his hand at work in what goes on. Life has its tough times, sometimes one after another. But if we continue to trust our God, even when light still has not appeared, he will show himself and the final outcome will be something we can look back on with thanksgiving.

Where are you at this moment? Setting out in hope for Moab? Experiencing disaster, way out there? On the weary path back? Labouring in the already-cut harvest field? Or giving thanks in the place of fulfilment? Many of you will be somewhere along that storyline today. And the good God knows and cares. Do not forget to bring him, by his name, into the picture and into your story.

Lord God, I think I'm like... at this moment. Please walk with me, wherever this road may lead and bring me to the best possible destination, I pray. In Jesus' name. Amen.

PAUL GRAVELLE

Water from the well

At that time David was on a fortified hill, and a group of Philistines had occupied Bethlehem. David grew homesick and said, 'How I wish someone would bring me a drink of water from the well by the gate at Bethlehem!' The three famous soldiers forced their way through the Philistine camp, drew some water from the well, and brought it back to David. But he would not drink it; instead, he poured it out as an offering to the Lord and said, 'Lord, I could never drink this! It would be like drinking the blood of these men who risked their lives!'

The Bethlehem region must have had good water as well as good fertile soil. Later, of course, it was to produce the water of life, as we have recently been celebrating (although the water, according to Jesus, was to be the Spirit, yet to be given; see John 3).

Neither the Apostles' Creed nor the Nicene Creed say much about the Holy Spirit. I think she deserves better than that. Did I say 'she'? Yes. I think that the notion of a female Holy Spirit balances the male gender of Father and Son appropriately. What do you think about that?

In recent times, God the Holy Spirit has become a bit forgotten, I feel. She (yes, I am sticking with that) is so important in refreshing, empowering and sustaining us in our Christian journey. The early Christians were like David's three famous soldiers. It pays to remember the early chapters of the Acts of the Apostles. They blazed the way, rushing on in the power of the Spirit and showing us how to grow a church. But I often feel we would be ashamed to show ourselves and some of our churches to them. The Holy Spirit has been the driving force of the church in every revival of faith down through the ages; 2025 could see another one if we are willing to draw water from the well.

---

*Holy Spirit, you have refreshed and empowered your church
to leap forward spectacularly many times in the past. Let this coming year
see such a time of renewal, we pray, and so refresh us
that we are ready to play our part in it. Amen.*

PAUL GRAVELLE

God's presence in the temples

'This is the command of Cyrus, Emperor of Persia. The Lord, the God of Heaven, has made me ruler over the whole world and has given me the responsibility of building a temple for him in Jerusalem in Judah… You are to go to Jerusalem and rebuild the temple of the Lord, the God of Israel'… Many of the exiles left the province of Babylon and returned to Jerusalem and Judah, all to their own hometowns… People whose ancestors had lived in the following towns also returned: a. Bethlehem – 123.

We have passed over the stories of David, in which Bethlehem figures large, and move now to the temple, which figures larger still in the Old Testament in different ways. Moses set up the tabernacle as a temporary temple – a location for the visible presence of God. Solomon's temple served the same obvious purpose (see 1 Kings 8:10–13), but the Babylonians destroyed it. A pathetic remnant claiming Bethlehemite descent were among those returning from exile to start the rebuild, but this second temple was never to house God's visible presence. A second scripture reading is helpful here because, early in his ministry, Jesus claimed that he himself was the temple, saying: 'Tear down this temple, and in three days I will build it again' (John 2:19).

Jesus was a Bethlehemite himself, of course. Joseph had returned to his home town for the census, and he became the head of a new Bethlehemite family almost as soon as he arrived. So Jesus' link to Bethlehem goes right back to Caleb, who represented the tribe of Judah (see Numbers 13). But Jesus' link to the tabernacle and to the first temple is far more important. He was God in the flesh: God's visible and touchable presence, a living temple in fact! Writing to the Gentile church in Ephesus, Paul said, 'You too are being built together with all the others into a place where God lives through his Spirit' (Ephesians 2:22).

Can you see that this turns those of us who have the Spirit of God into a temple? Wherever we are in the world, we are a temple where others may discover the very presence of God.

Pray that God prepares you for this to become a reality.

PAUL GRAVELLE

Jeremiah's prophecy of hope.

The Lord Almighty, the God of Israel, says, 'When I restore the people to their land, they will once again say in the land of Judah and in its towns, "May the Lord bless the sacred hill of Jerusalem, the holy place where he lives." People will live in Judah and in all its towns, and there will be farmers, and shepherds with their flocks. I will refresh those who are weary and will satisfy with food everyone who is weak from hunger. So then, people will say, "I went to sleep and woke up refreshed."'

Jeremiah is not renowned for hopeful prophecy, but here is one which includes Bethlehem – one of the towns of Judah which, as we have seen, was located in a prosperous agricultural area. This was spoken before Israel was taken into captivity by Babylon, so it would later have been a comfort to those longing for the day of return.

How does the future look to you? Looking forward to 2025, what are the prospects for peace, climate, housing, health, immigration and many other matters of concern? Will you honestly be able to wish others 'Happy New Year'?

I write this in August 2023. My medical prognosis says that I am unlikely to see 2024, let alone 2025. I was able to say to the medical staff, 'I know where I am going.' I will be one of those who say, 'I went to sleep and woke up refreshed.' This is the prospect for those who believe in the Lord Jesus Christ, isn't it? But, for most of you who believe, 2025 will bring the usual run of problems and difficulties with family, with finances, with health, with the world and lots more. There is no end to that side of living.

But the same Lord Almighty truly remains in charge over all of his universe. He is still numbering every hair on your head; yes, even if there are none there! And he really is the loving one who is concerned about everything that is going to concern you in 2025.

See the interview with Paul, and the editor's note, on page 147.

Loving God, walk with me through 2025. Refresh me when I am weary and satisfy me when I am weak, I pray. For Jesus' sake. Amen.

PAUL GRAVELLE

Enjoy a little luxury: upgrade to *New Daylight deluxe*

Many readers enjoy the compact format of the regular *New Daylight* but more and more people are discovering the advantages of the larger format, premium edition, *New Daylight deluxe*. The pocket-sized version is perfect if you're reading on the move but the larger print, white paper and extra space to write your own notes and comments all make the deluxe edition an attractive alternative and significant upgrade.

Why not try it to see if you like it? You can order single copies at **brfonline.org.uk/newdaylightdeluxe**

Deluxe actual size:

gladness instead of mourning, the mantle of **spirit. They will be called oaks of righteous**ness, **to display his glory.**

We learn from these verses that gladness is first them' gladness instead of mourning and praise in gift needs to be received, and action is often req gift. For example, receiving a piano is of little us play it. God has blessed us with 'every spiritual but, metaphorically speaking, *we* have to pour o put on and wear the mantle of praise. The Lord

SHARING OUR VISION – MAKING A GIFT

I would like to make a donation to support BRF Ministries.
Please use my gift for:

☐ Where the need is greatest   ☐ Anna Chaplaincy   ☐ Living Faith

☐ Messy Church   ☐ Parenting for Faith

Title	First name/initials	Surname	
Address			
			Postcode
Email			
Telephone			
Signature			Date

Our ministry is only possible because of the generous support of individuals, churches, trusts and gifts in wills.

Please treat as Gift Aid donations all qualifying gifts of money made *(tick all that apply)*

giftaid it

☐ today,   ☐ in the past four years,   ☐ and in the future.

I am a UK taxpayer and understand that if I pay less Income Tax and/or Capital Gains Tax in the current tax year than the amount of Gift Aid claimed on all my donations, it is my responsibility to pay any difference.

☐ My donation does not qualify for Gift Aid.

Please notify us if you want to cancel this Gift Aid declaration, change your name or home address, or no longer pay sufficient tax on your income and/or capital gains.

You can also give online at **brf.org.uk/donate**, which reduces our administration costs, making your donation go further.

Please complete other side of form ➲

SHARING OUR VISION – MAKING A GIFT

Please accept my gift of:

☐ £2 ☐ £5 ☐ £10 ☐ £20 Other £ [   ]

by (*delete as appropriate*):

☐ Cheque/Charity Voucher payable to 'BRF'

☐ MasterCard/Visa/Debit card/Charity card

Name on card

Card no. [ ][ ][ ][ ] [ ][ ][ ][ ] [ ][ ][ ][ ] [ ][ ][ ][ ]

Expires end [M][M] [Y][Y] Security code* [ ][ ][ ] *Last 3 digits on the reverse of the card

Signature   Date

☐ I would like to leave a gift to BRF Ministries in my will.
   Please send me further information.

☐ I would like to find out about giving a regular gift to BRF Ministries.

For help or advice regarding making a gift, please contact
our fundraising team **+44 (0)1865 462305**

Your privacy

We will use your personal data to process this transaction.
From time to time we may send you information about
the work of BRF Ministries that we think may be of
interest to you. Our privacy policy is available at
brf.org.uk/privacy. Please contact us if you wish to
discuss your mailing preferences.

Registered with

FUNDRAISING
REGULATOR

↻ Please complete other side of form

Please return this form to 'Freepost BRF'
No other address information or stamp is needed

Bible Reading Fellowship is a charity (233280) and company limited by guarantee (301324),
registered in England and Wales

Reading *New Daylight* in a group

GORDON GILES

It is good to talk. While the Rule of Benedict recommends daily scripture reading as a key aspect of the community life of work and prayer, discussion and reflection are a good consequence of reading passages that others are reading simultaneously. Separated by space, as each reads alone, we are yet connected by the common food of scripture, taken in our own time at our own pace. We each chew on it in our own way.

Yet discussion or shared reflection on the passages chosen and the comments made can aid digestion, so here are some 'open' questions that may enable discussion in a Bible study or other group who gather to take further what is published here. The same questions may also inform the silence of personal devotion too. Use them as you wish and may God bless and inspire you on your journey as you read, mark and inwardly digest holy words to ponder and nourish the soul.

General discussion starters

These can be used for any study series within this issue. Remember there are no right or wrong answers – these questions are simply to enable a group to engage in conversation.

- What do you think is the main idea or theme of the author in this series? Did that come across strongly?
- Have any of the issues discussed touched on personal – or shared – aspects of your life?
- What evidence or stories do the authors draw on to illuminate, or be illuminated by, the passages of scripture?
- Which do you prefer: scripture informing daily modern life, or modern life shining a new light on scripture?
- Does the author 'call you to action' in a realistic and achievable way? Do you think their ideas will work in the secular world?
- Have any specific passages struck you personally? If so, how and why? Is God speaking to you through scripture and reflection?
- Was anything completely new to you? Any 'eureka' or jaw-dropping moments? If so, what difference will that make?

Questions for group discussion

Proverbs 25—29 (Margaret Silf)

- The style of these texts tends to be very 'black and white'. In practice, life is not so simple and requires much compromise and the ability to discern the better way forward from among many choices. How do you respond to some of the writer's simple oppositions?

- These wisdom sayings assume that God always blesses wisdom and condemns foolishness. We know that, in this life, this rarely appears to be the case. Can we trust that on a higher plane of being, that we cannot yet imagine, this reflects a greater truth?

- The writer has a great deal to say about justice. How do these repeated calls for justice resonate with our global and national situations today?

- How do these texts challenge us to examine closely and critically those who hold authority in our societies today, but also our own conduct and decisions in any roles of leadership to which we ourselves are called, whether in the family or the wider world?

- Of the several challenges to our values and conduct held out to us in the readings of these two weeks, which do you feel most urgently apply to our situation in today's turbulent world?

Parables in Mark (Veronica Zundel)

- Why do you think Jesus told parables?

- In an industrial, non-agrarian society, what image might you substitute for the repeated image of a sown seed and its growth?

- Can you think of examples where the church is learning to put new wine in new wineskins? Or failing to do so?

- Jesus told us, 'You are the light of the world' (Matthew 5:14). How can we let the light of our faith shine without being like the Pharisees, parading our superiority?

- In what ways have you experienced God's abundant provision?

- What can we do in our churches to avoid putting 'stumbling blocks' in the way of the 'little ones'?

Matthew 8—9 (Gordon Giles)

- Why do you think Jesus performed miracles?

- Imagine a world without our medicine, mental health care or knowledge – how must these miracles of Jesus have struck the people present?

- What insights into first-century Palestinian life do these pericopes give us? Would you have liked to have lived then – or is our world barely different or better?

- What can the word 'healing' mean? What is your favourite definition?

- Is there any connection between healing and sin? Is such a connection helpful, dangerous, or irrelevant?

- Do we need miracles or deeds of power today? Have you encountered any? Share stories and examples.

The return of Christ (Margot and Martin Hodson)

- Will we be able to tell when Jesus is going to return?

- What are the 'mechanics' of the return of Christ? What will the consequences be?

- How does the promised 'new heaven and new earth' play out in practice? Does it involve a destruction of the present order or a renewal of it?

- How should we live in the light of the impending return of Jesus?

- How can we take the judgement of Christ seriously?

- How do we relate events such as wars, natural disasters and ecological concerns (such as climate change) that happen in our age to an understanding of the 'end times'?

Meet the author: Paul Gravelle

It is with sadness, but also with resurrection hope, that we inform readers that Paul died in November 2023. He had been a contributor to New Daylight for several years and was able to write a further set of notes, which will be published next year. So we will hear from him again, but for the time being we commend him to our Lord Jesus, giving thanks for his ministry which spread across the globe through his writing. Our thoughts and our prayers are with his wife Janice and his family. May he rest in peace and rise in glory.

How did you come to faith and what were the earliest influences on your Christian journey?

My early life was a Bible-soaked experience, for which I am most grateful. But it was also very puritanical and, in my teens, I rejected both that and the very cross-focused emphasis that went with it. Church music kept me going to church, however, and coming to New Zealand from the UK in 1964, I found faith through charismatic renewal. I met with Jesus when I was filled with the Holy Spirit under Fr Dennis Bennet's ministry and have never been the same from that moment!

Tell us about where you live, your church context and ministry?

I was ordained priest in 1975 and served in a remote rural district for four years. My first wife then died tragically from spinal cancer, and I returned to Auckland, serving as officiating chaplain to the Royal New Zealand Air Force (RNZAF). I remarried, and Janice and I had years of fun with a blended family of teenagers. We now live in a wonderful retirement village on the shores of Auckland's Waitemata Harbour, and I have been licenced as priest assistant at Northwest Anglican Church of the Good Shepherd since 1983.

What have been the greatest joys and sadnesses of your life and ministry?

In the 1970s and early 1980s I conducted countless 'Life in the Spirit' seminars. This was the most rewarding and most joyful period of my ministry. In 1975 I was ordained deacon, and then priest in 1977. The gap represents the greatest sadness in my life, when I found myself confronting what I can only describe as unholy influences in the church at that time. I have always supported myself. That has been my calling and, for some people, self-supported ministry seems to be more acceptable.

What is your favourite book of the Bible and why?

John's gospel every time! From 3:16 onwards, John portrays Jesus calling people to believe – believe who he is. It is this belief that brings us eternal life, he says. It was this belief that marked early Christians coming for baptism. 'Jesus Christ is Lord,' they proclaimed – and eternal life was theirs. There is always more to learn as we walk with Jesus, but the walk can only begin when we believe who it is with whom we are walking. John is the biblical writer who emphasises this truth so powerfully.

If you could advise a younger generation what would you say to them?

The younger generation are entirely open to thinking beyond space and time. I would first want to introduce them to the real Jesus – who he is, the man who is actually God in a human body. I would then ask the Holy Spirit to demonstrate her presence in whatever way she chose, so that the truth of who Jesus is might be verified by some simple supernatural event of the kind often experienced in Christian circles. I would challenge them to believe – and then to believe even more and to follow. But believing comes first!

Recommended reading

God became flesh at Christmas. But how does God, who created all things, live within the limitations of humanity – limitations that humanity itself often resents and tries to transcend? And what does it truly mean to be human? As contemporary society grapples with questions of identity, justice and medical ethics, *Embracing Humanity* deftly explores how different aspects of being human are both inhabited and transformed in the incarnation.

Through the lens of Advent and Christmas, Isabelle Hamley guides us through daily reflections and prayers, encouraging us to meditate on being human in the light of God's choice to reach out to us in Jesus.

The following is an edited extract taken from the Introduction.

I grew up in a world without Christmas.

As a child in a virulently atheist family, going through the highly secular French education system, I simply did not hear the story of Christmas until I was a teenager. Of course, we had a tree and presents, and as an avid reader I came across rumours of Christmas in books, but nothing concrete or explicit. Christmas was just a cultural artefact, a time to get presents and endure distant relatives. Magic and wonder waned as soon as I stopped believing in Father Christmas (no mention of 'Santa' in my family, that would have been far too religious).

Watching my first nativity, age twelve, was a revelation. The sheer wonder of it still gives me goosebumps: the hard journey, the promise of a star, the extraordinary baby unrecognised while an indifferent world goes by. I still love nativities. In particular, I love school nativities. They're a wonderful, chaotic, odd take on the Christmas story. Sometimes they are so chaotic it is actually difficult to recognise much of the Christmas story in there, in between unicorns, aliens and robots. I love them, because they tug on a familiar story – after all, even in the weirdest, most outlandish interpretations, you still have Mary, Joseph and Jesus, and the wonder of the birth. At the same time, they bring in so much else – all the strange, quirky aspects of our humanity, with joy and celebration that we can't always explain, and the occasional bun fight between ox and donkey. School nativities are a cacophony of humanity. And this is the world, the people God has come to walk with, in their habits and cultures and choices, even the questionable ones.

Even when the message passes by those gathered, focused as they are on taking pictures of their own little cherubs dressed in makeshift donkey costumes, nevertheless, in this echo of the story, there is something of God-with-us, still often unrecognised, but present nonetheless. There is still something of God coming into the reality of our lives, right in the midst of them, and taking shape in the particularities of where we are. Christmas points us to who God is, but it also points us towards what it means to be human and how God chooses to become one of us.

The 21st century is a strange time to be human. Today rumours are not of God-made-flesh, but of artificial intelligence, which may make many humans redundant. God became flesh, but human beings seem constantly eager to escape being flesh: we make disincarnated, disembodied 'intelligence', in our image. We try to flee our bodies in virtual reality, and modern medicine gives us ways to change the bodies we do not like or want and prolong life far beyond previously natural ends. What can the Christmas story tell us about who we are in this changing world? What does it mean for the Good News to be good news for the whole human person, rather than just minds or souls? Who are we called to be, as we walk with the God who walks with us?

To be a Christian is to believe that God, the creator of the universe, is beyond anything we can imagine or fathom. Yet it is also to believe that this God, who created us, stooped to earth and chose to become one of us. It is to believe that in God's eyes, our humanity is not something to transcend, but something to embrace.

This Advent, I invite you on a journey to explore humanity in the light of Jesus' coming. Each day, we will explore a different aspect of Jesus' humanity, of God's wholehearted embrace of the world he created. Humanity is not an easy thing to live with; we often struggle with our limitations, and the realities of a physical world we cannot ever fully control, and a human world of interactions that brings as much pain as it brings joy. And yet this is the existence that God chose and embraced. God brought salvation not by removing us from our humanity, but by entering it, and inviting us into a journey of transformation within it.

To order

Online: brfonline.org.uk
Telephone: +44 (0)1865 319700
Mon–Fri 9.30–17.00

Delivery times within the UK are
normally 15 working days. Prices are
correct at the time of going to press
but may change without prior notice.

Title	Price	Qty	Total
A Calendar of Carols	£9.99		
Image of the Invisible	£8.99		
Images of Grace	£9.99		
Embracing Humanity – BRF Advent book	£9.99		
The Poetry of Pilgrimage	£12.99		

POSTAGE AND PACKING CHARGES			
Order value	UK	Europe	Rest of world
Under £7.00	£2.00		
£7.00–£29.99	£3.00	Available on request	Available on request
£30.00 and over	FREE		

Total value of books	
Postage and packing	
Donation*	
Total for this order	

* Please complete and return the
Gift Aid declaration on page 141.

Please complete in BLOCK CAPITALS

Title .... First name/initials .... Surname..................................

Address..

.... Postcode ....

Acc. No. .... Telephone ....

Email..

Method of payment

☐ Cheque (made payable to BRF) ☐ MasterCard / Visa

Card no. [ ][ ][ ][ ] [ ][ ][ ][ ] [ ][ ][ ][ ] [ ][ ][ ][ ]

Expires end [M][M] [Y][Y]   Security code [ ][ ][ ]   Last 3 digits on the reverse
of the card

We will use your personal data to process this order. From time to time we may send you information
about the work of BRF Ministries. Please contact us if you wish to discuss your mailing preferences. Our
privacy policy is available at **brf.org.uk/privacy**.

Please return this form to:

BRF Ministries, 15 The Chambers, Vineyard, Abingdon OX14 3FE | **enquiries@brf.org.uk**
For terms and cancellation information, please visit **brfonline.org.uk/terms**.

Bible Reading Fellowship (BRF) is a charity (233280) and company limited by guarantee (301324),
registered in England and Wales

BRF Ministries needs you!

If you're one of our many thousands of regular *New Daylight* readers you will know all about the rich rewards of regular Bible reading and the value of daily notes to guide, inform and inspire you. Here are some recent comments from *New Daylight* readers:

'Thank you for all the many inspiring writings that help so much when things are tough.'

'Just right for me – I learned a lot!'

'We looked forward to each day's message as we pondered each passage and comment.'

If you have similarly positive things to say about *New Daylight*, would you be willing to help spread the word about these popular resources? Could you follow the example of long-standing *New Daylight* reader Beryl Fudge and form a *New Daylight* reading group, not to take the place of private prayer and reading but to share insights and deepen understanding. 'I've quite a few friends who also take the notes and we discuss them in the group,' says Beryl: '... there's so much in them every day. What I most value in *New Daylight* is the way that they connect the Old and New Testament scriptures with what's happening here and now.'

It doesn't need to be complicated: every issue of *New Daylight* includes questions for reflection or discussion.

We can supply further information if you need it and would love to hear about it if you do form a *New Daylight* reading group.

For more information:

- Email **enquiries@brf.org.uk**
- Phone us on **+44 (0)1865 319700** Mon–Fri 9.30–17.00
- Write to us at BRF Ministries, 15 The Chambers, Vineyard, Abingdon OX14 3FE

Inspiring people of all ages to grow in Christian faith

BRF Ministries

At BRF Ministries, we long for people of all ages to grow in faith and understanding of the Bible. That's what all our work as a charity is about.

- Our **Living Faith** range of resources helps Christians go deeper in their understanding of scripture, in prayer and in their walk with God. Our conferences and events bring people together to share this journey, while our Holy Habits resources help whole congregations grow together as disciples of Jesus, living out and sharing their faith.

- We also want to make it easier for local churches to engage effectively in ministry and mission – by helping them bring new families into a growing relationship with God through **Messy Church** or by supporting churches as they nurture the spiritual life of older people through **Anna Chaplaincy**.

- Our **Parenting for Faith** team coaches parents and others to raise God-connected children and teens, and enables churches to fully support them.

Do you share our vision?

Though a significant proportion of BRF Ministries' funding is generated through our charitable activities, we are dependent on the generous support of individuals, churches and charitable trusts.

If you share our vision, would you help us to inspire even more people of all ages to grow in Christian faith? Your prayers and financial support are vital for the work that we do. You could:

- support us with a regular donation or one-off gift
- consider leaving a gift to BRF Ministries in your will
- encourage your church to support us as part of your church's giving to home mission – perhaps focusing on a specific ministry or programme
- most important of all, support us with your prayers.

Donate at **brf.org.uk/donate** or use the form on pages 141–42.

Alpha and Omega

'Look, I am coming soon! My reward is with me, and I will give to each person according to what they have done. I am the Alpha and the Omega, the First and the Last, the Beginning and the End.'

REVELATION 22:12–13 (NIV)

As this set of notes begins in September, Christmas feels very far away. Many activities are starting up again after the summer and for some this brings changes both large and small.

Our Messy Church team are on hand as people start using the new sessions from *Get Messy! Volume 2* and supporting them through the continuing series of Masterclasses. Meanwhile, the Living Faith team are hard at work enabling people to access our Advent collection, and are preparing books and resources to add to our Lent collection in the new year.

Our Parenting for Faith team begin another cycle of their training courses, equipping parents and others to support their children in faith from the cradle into adulthood. The Anna Chaplaincy team continue supporting our ever-growing network as they work with our elderly community, shedding welcome and needed light as the nights grow darker and the year comes to its glorious end with the coming of Christ at Christmas.

We want to keep inspiring people to grow in their Christian faith; after all, this is the mission we remain rooted to. Our work would not be possible without kind donations from individuals, churches, charitable trusts and gifts in wills. If you would like to support us now and in the future you can become a Friend of BRF Ministries by making a monthly gift of £2 a month or more – we thank you for your friendship.

Find out more at **brf.org.uk/donate** or get in touch with us on **01235 462305** or via **giving@brf.org.uk**

The fundraising team at BRF Ministries

NEW DAYLIGHT SUBSCRIPTION RATES

Please note our new subscription rates, current until 30 April 2025:

Individual subscriptions
covering 3 issues for under 5 copies, payable in advance
(including postage & packing):

	UK	Europe	Rest of world
New Daylight	£19.50	£26.85	£30.75
New Daylight 3-year subscription (9 issues) (not available for Deluxe)	£57.60	N/A	N/A
New Daylight Deluxe per set of 3 issues p.a.	£24.75	£33.15	£39.15

Group subscriptions
covering 3 issues for 5 copies or more, sent to one UK address (post free):

New Daylight	£14.97 per set of 3 issues p.a.
New Daylight Deluxe	£19.05 per set of 3 issues p.a.

Please note that the annual billing period for group subscriptions runs from 1 May to 30 April.

Overseas group subscription rates
Available on request. Please email **enquiries@brf.org.uk**.

Copies may also be obtained from Christian bookshops:

New Daylight	£4.99 per copy
New Daylight Deluxe	£6.35 per copy

> All our Bible reading notes can be ordered online
> by visiting **brfonline.org.uk/subscriptions**

NEW DAYLIGHT INDIVIDUAL SUBSCRIPTION FORM

All our Bible reading notes can be ordered online by visiting
brfonline.org.uk/subscriptions

Title .... First name/initials .... Surname ....

Address ....

.... Postcode ....

Telephone .... Email ....

Please send *New Daylight* beginning with the January 2025 / May 2025 /
September 2025 issue (*delete as appropriate*):

(*please tick box*)	UK	Europe	Rest of world
New Daylight 1-year subscription	☐ £19.50	☐ £26.85	☐ £30.75
New Daylight 3-year subscription	☐ £57.60	N/A	N/A
New Daylight Deluxe	☐ £24.75	☐ £33.15	☐ £39.15

Optional donation to support the work of BRF Ministries £ ....

Total enclosed £ .... (cheques should be made payable to 'BRF')

Please complete and return the Gift Aid declaration on page 141 to make your
donation even more valuable to us.

Please charge my MasterCard / Visa with £ ....

Card no. ☐☐☐☐ ☐☐☐☐ ☐☐☐☐ ☐☐☐☐

Expires end M M Y Y Security code ☐☐☐ Last 3 digits on the reverse of the card

To set up a Direct Debit, please complete the Direct Debit instruction on page 159.

We will use your personal data to process this order. From time to time we may send you
information about the work of BRF Ministries. Please contact us if you wish to discuss your
mailing preferences. Our privacy policy is available at **brf.org.uk/privacy**.

Please return this form with the appropriate payment to:
BRF Ministries, 15 The Chambers, Vineyard, Abingdon OX14 3FE
For terms and cancellation information, please visit **brfonline.org.uk/terms**.

Bible Reading Fellowship is a charity (233280) and company limited by guarantee (301324),
registered in England and Wales

ND0324

NEW DAYLIGHT GIFT SUBSCRIPTION FORM

☐ I would like to give a gift subscription (please provide both names and addresses):

Title .... First name/initials .... Surname ....

Address ....

.... Postcode ....

Telephone .... Email ....

Gift subscription name ....

Gift subscription address ....

.... Postcode ....

Gift message (20 words max. or include your own gift card):

....

....

Please send *New Daylight* beginning with the January 2025 / May 2025 / September 2025 issue (*delete as appropriate*):

(*please tick box*)

	UK	Europe	Rest of world
New Daylight 1-year subscription	☐ £19.50	☐ £26.85	☐ £30.75
New Daylight 3-year subscription	☐ £57.60	N/A	N/A
New Daylight Deluxe	☐ £24.75	☐ £33.15	☐ £39.15

Optional donation to support the work of BRF Ministries £ ....

Total enclosed £ .... (cheques should be made payable to 'BRF')

Please complete and return the Gift Aid declaration on page 141 to make your donation even more valuable to us.

Please charge my MasterCard / Visa with £ ....

Card no. ☐☐☐☐ ☐☐☐☐ ☐☐☐☐ ☐☐☐☐

Expires end ☐☐ ☐☐ Security code ☐☐☐ Last 3 digits on the reverse of the card

To set up a Direct Debit, please complete the Direct Debit instruction on page 159.

We will use your personal data to process this order. From time to time we may send you information about the work of BRF Ministries. Please contact us if you wish to discuss your mailing preferences. Our privacy policy is available at **brf.org.uk/privacy**.

Please return this form with the appropriate payment to:
BRF Ministries, 15 The Chambers, Vineyard, Abingdon OX14 3FE
For terms and cancellation information, please visit **brfonline.org.uk/terms**.

Bible Reading Fellowship is a charity (233280) and company limited by guarantee (301324), registered in England and Wales

DIRECT DEBIT PAYMENT

You can pay for your annual subscription to our Bible reading notes using Direct Debit. You need only give your bank details once, and the payment is made automatically every year until you cancel it. If you would like to pay by Direct Debit, please use the form opposite, entering your BRF account number under 'Reference number'.

You are fully covered by the Direct Debit Guarantee:

The Direct Debit Guarantee

- This Guarantee is offered by all banks and building societies that accept instructions to pay Direct Debits.

- If there are any changes to the amount, date or frequency of your Direct Debit, Bible Reading Fellowship will notify you 10 working days in advance of your account being debited or as otherwise agreed. If you request Bible Reading Fellowship to collect a payment, confirmation of the amount and date will be given to you at the time of the request.

- If an error is made in the payment of your Direct Debit, by Bible Reading Fellowship or your bank or building society, you are entitled to a full and immediate refund of the amount paid from your bank or building society.

- If you receive a refund you are not entitled to, you must pay it back when Bible Reading Fellowship asks you to.

- You can cancel a Direct Debit at any time by simply contacting your bank or building society. Written confirmation may be required. Please also notify us.

Instruction to your bank or building society to pay by Direct Debit

Please fill in the whole form using a ballpoint pen and return with order form to:
BRF Ministries, 15 The Chambers, Vineyard, Abingdon OX14 3FE

Service User Number: | 5 | 5 | 8 | 2 | 2 | 9 |

Name and full postal address of your bank or building society

To: The Manager	Bank/Building Society
Address	
	Postcode

Name(s) of account holder(s)

Branch sort code

| | | - | | | - | | | |

Bank/Building Society account number

| | | | | | | | |

Reference number

| | | | | | | | |

Instruction to your Bank/Building Society
Please pay Bible Reading Fellowship Direct Debits from the account detailed in this instruction, subject to the safeguards assured by the Direct Debit Guarantee. I understand that this instruction may remain with Bible Reading Fellowship and, if so, details will be passed electronically to my bank/building society.

Signature(s)

Banks and Building Societies may not accept Direct Debit instructions for some types of account.

BRF Ministries

Inspiring people of all ages to grow in Christian faith

BRF Ministries is the home of Anna Chaplaincy, Living Faith, Messy Church and Parenting for Faith

As a charity, our work would not be possible without fundraising and gifts in wills.

To find out more and to donate, visit brf.org.uk/give or call +44 (0)1235 462305

Registered with
FUNDRAISING
REGULATOR